Teradata Physical Design and Implementation

An Authorized Teradata Certified Professional Program Study Guide

Exam TE0-143

First Edition

ISBN 978-0-9894005-1-0
Printed by Cerulium Corporation

Stephen Wilmes
Eric Rivard

Copyright

Trademarks

Special Acknowledgement

A special thank you to the following individuals that contributed to the Study Guide content: Susan Hahn, Michael McBride, David Micheletto, Jim Petruzzelli, and Larry Rex.

About the Author - Steve Wilmes

Steve Wilmes founded Cerulium Corporation in 2007. As Chief Executive Officer, his goal is to establish Cerulium as a premier data warehousing Technology Company. Cerulium's strategic growth is globally focused on six lines of business including education, consulting, BI solutions, productivity tools, application integration and assessment services. These lines of business have been highly successful by utilizing strategic data warehousing solutions provided by Teradata that spans across the consumer, and commercial markets.

Mr. Wilmes has over 20 years of experience in the computer industry and is known to be a detail-oriented, results-focused leader. He is an internationally recognized expert in several aspects of data warehousing including hardware, software, SQL, operating systems, implementation, data integration, database administration, and BI solutions.

Mr. Wilmes earned a bachelor's degree in business administration and economics from Augsburg College and he is also a Teradata Certified Master.

Mr. Wilmes resides just outside of Columbia, South Carolina, with his wife, Becky. He has been involved with numerous civic, educational, and business organizations throughout his career. Some of his more recent associations include working with the Richland County Sheriff's Department – Region 4 Community Member, and volunteer for local organizations where he shares his technical expertise.

About the Author - Eric Rivard

Eric Rivard is the COO and Vice President of Cerulium Corporation, and is responsible for consulting and product development operations. Mr. Rivard has substantial industry experience across the telecommunications, retail, and healthcare industries, and has consulted at many Fortune 500 companies. His in-depth knowledge of the Teradata platform has enabled him to design and develop customized Teradata applications. He has worked with some of the largest data warehouses in the world, providing unique software solutions and solving complex business problems.

Mr. Rivard dedicated the bulk of his career to the pursuit of data heterogeneity. Outside of this Teradata expertise, he worked extensively with a variety of database platforms, and developed software products that integrate across the different RDBMS systems. He is an experienced Microsoft .NET developer, which has enabled him to use Microsoft's best-in-class development tools as a foundation for Cerulium Corporation's data warehouse applications.

Mr. Rivard resides just outside of Atlanta, Georgia, with his wife, Susana, and their three children. Outside of his professional career, he is actively involved in many community activities. In addition, he serves on the Advisory Board for the Management Information Systems (MIS) program at his alma mater, the Terry College of Business at the University of Georgia, where he earned his Bachelor of Business Administration in MIS and International Business.

Table of Contents

Chapter 1: The Teradata Certified Professional Program

Pursue Teradata Certification with Confidence™

The Teradata Certified Professional Program (TCPP), launched in 1999, develops and manages Teradata's premier, and only, certification testing program. Teradata authorized training and proctored exams, available globally to customers, partners, associates, and students, are instrumental in establishing an industry-standard measure of technical competence for IT professionals using Teradata technology. Recognized as a leader in Data Warehouse RDBMS technology and valued by major global companies using Teradata, more than 57,000 Teradata Certifications have been awarded.

The new Teradata 14 Certification Track consists of seven exams that combine for achievement of six certifications and provides a logical progression for specific job roles. Starting with the core Teradata 14 Certified Professional credential, individuals have an opportunity to demonstrate knowledge by achieving Certification as a Technical Specialist, Database Administrator, Solutions Developer, Enterprise Architect, and the most prestigious Teradata Certification – Teradata 14 Certified Master.

The purpose of this Certification Exam Study Guide is to assist you with your goal to become Teradata Certified. This Guide will provide focused content areas, high level explanations around the key areas of focus, and help you to determine areas of further study prior to sitting for the Teradata Certification examination.

Although the Exam Study Guide will assist you in exam preparation, you must be knowledgeable of the subject areas in order to pass the exam. This Guide is intended for individuals who have completed the recommended training and have the recommended amount of

Teradata experience. **We do not guarantee that you will pass the exam simply by reading the Exam Study Guide.** Only hard work, hands-on experience, and a positive attitude will help you to achieve exam success. We wish you the very best of luck!

"When hiring, I always look for Teradata Certified Professionals. Not only does it provide me a good understanding of a candidate's knowledge level, it also shows a commitment to continuous learning and self-improvement. That's a great trait to have in every employee and the Teradata Certified Professional Program makes it easy to recognize."
Teradata Certified Master, Insurance Industry

The flowchart and matrix below are designed to help you define a path to the knowledge, skills, and experience needed to achieve Teradata 14 Certifications.

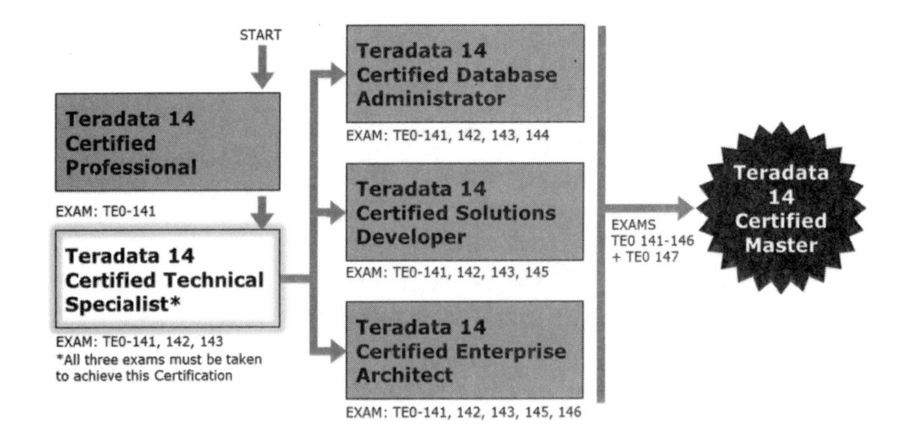

Your Teradata 14 Certification Upgrade Roadmap

Teradata 12 Certified candidates, in good standing, are eligible to take the *Teradata 14 Bridge from Teradata 12 Exam (TE0-14B).* The Bridge exam is a hybrid of all three (3) Teradata baseline Certification exams,

and covers content changes to Teradata Basics, Teradata SQL and Teradata Physical Design & Implementation exams.
A passed exam result on the Bridge exam will yield the *Teradata 14 Certified Technical Specialist* designation. A candidate may then continue on the Teradata 14 track until achieving the desired Certification level.

Teradata 14 Certifications	
Teradata 14 Certified Professional	
Exams Required: • TE0-141 – Teradata 14 Basics Must be passed before continuing on certification path	Recommended Teradata Experience: 6-12 months Recommended Preparation Courses: • Introduction to the Teradata Database
Teradata 14 Certified Technical Specialist	
Exams Required: • TE0-141 – Teradata 14 Basics • TE0-142 – Teradata 14 SQL • TE0-143 – Teradata 14 Physical Design and Implementation 3 Exams to be passed in sequential order	Recommended Teradata Experience: 1-2 years Recommended Preparation Courses: • Introduction to the Teradata Database • Teradata SQL • Advanced Teradata SQL • Physical Database Design • Physical Database Tuning

Teradata 14 Certified Database Administrator

Exams Required:
- TE0-141 – Teradata 14 Basics
- TE0-142 – Teradata 14 SQL
- TE0-143 – Teradata 14 Physical Design and Implementation
- TE0-144 – Teradata 14 Database Administration

4 Exams to be passed in sequential order

Recommended Teradata Experience:
2-3 years

Recommended Preparation Courses:
- Introduction to the Teradata Database
- Teradata SQL
- Advanced Teradata SQL
- Physical Database Design
- Physical Database Tuning
- Teradata Application Utilities
- Teradata Parallel Transporter
- Teradata Warehouse Management
- Teradata Warehouse Administration

Teradata 14 Certified Solutions Developer

Exams Required:
- TE0-141 – Teradata 14 Basics
- TE0-142 – Teradata 14 SQL
- TE0-143 – Teradata 14 Physical Design and Implementation
- TE0-145 – Teradata 14 Solutions Development

4 Exams to be passed in sequential order

Recommended Teradata Experience:
2-3 years

Recommended Preparation Courses:
- Introduction to the Teradata Database
- Teradata SQL
- Advanced Teradata SQL
- Physical Database Design
- Physical Database Tuning
- Teradata Application Utilities
- Teradata Parallel Transporter
- Teradata Application Design and Development

Teradata 14 Certified Enterprise Architect

Exams Required:

- TE0-141 – Teradata 14 Basics
- TE0-142 – Teradata 14 SQL
- TE0-143 – Teradata 14 Physical Design and Implementation
- TE0-145 – Teradata 14 Solutions Development
- TE0-146 – Teradata 14 Enterprise Architecture

5 Exams to be passed in sequential order

Recommended Teradata Experience:

2-3 years

Recommended Preparation Courses:

- Introduction to the Teradata Database
- Teradata SQL
- Advanced Teradata SQL
- Physical Database Design
- Physical Database Tuning
- Teradata Application Utilities
- Teradata Parallel Transporter
- Teradata Warehouse Management
- Teradata Warehouse Administration
- Teradata Application Design and Development

Teradata 14 Certified Master*

Exams Required:

- TE0-141 - TE0-146: Successful completion of all exams **PLUS:**
- TE0-147 – Teradata 14 Comprehensive Mastery Exam

7 Exams to be passed in sequential order

*Path for Teradata 12 Certified Masters

- TE0-147 – Teradata 14 Comprehensive Mastery Exam

Recommended Teradata Experience:

A minimum 5 years practical hands-on experience is highly recommended

Recommended Preparation Courses:

- Introduction to the Teradata Database
- Teradata SQL
- Advanced Teradata SQL
- Physical Database Design
- Physical Database Tuning
- Teradata Application Utilities
- Teradata Parallel Transporter
- Teradata Warehouse Management
- Teradata Warehouse Administration
- Teradata Application Design and Development

Note: Formal education recommendations may vary based on previous training and relevant job experience.

Certification... Knowledge Building to Mastery

Competition is fierce. Differentiate yourself while building critical IT technology knowledge and skills. Trust Teradata Certification to help you build the expertise employers are looking for in a demanding, data-driven global business environment. Teradata developed a new generation of certification exams that bring premium value to Teradata 14 Certification credentials.

Top 10 "What's new about the Teradata 14 Certification Track?"

1. Seven exams with all new content based upon the following database releases: Teradata Database 13.0, Teradata Database 13.1, Teradata Database 14.0 (including SLES 11)
2. The "*Teradata 14 Bridge from Teradata 12*" Exam allows Teradata 12 certified candidates to move, or "bridge", from the Teradata 12 Certification track to the Teradata 14 Certification track without starting the track from the beginning.
3. Eligibility-based exams to ensure compliance with Teradata Certification requirements (Bridge and Masters exams only)
4. Teradata 12 Certified Masters will take just one exam to update to Teradata 14 Certified Master status.
5. A Qualification exam is not required for those that have achieved a Teradata 12 Master Certification.
6. A new Candidate Agreement and revised security measures are in place to protect the value of your investment and integrity of all exams and certifications.
7. Newly designed electronic certificates, wallet cards, and logos.
8. An easy Certification verification process for individuals and employers.
9. More rigorous certification criteria including a combination of training, study, and practical, hands-on experience.

10. A team of dedicated, experienced, and knowledgeable individuals with a passion to help you achieve your Teradata Certification goals!

Path to Teradata 14 Mastery

A Teradata Certified Master enjoys a distinct advantage in the global marketplace. Employers seek Teradata Certified staff with verifiable knowledge and skills that support their business-critical Teradata systems. The TCPP process helps those individuals who want to deepen their knowledge and build their skills to the highest level.

The path to achieve Teradata 14 Certified Master status is summarized in the matrix below.

If You Are...	Exams Required for Teradata 14 Master Certification
Starting on the Teradata 14 Certification Track	• TE0-141 – TE0-147 All 7 Exams required
Teradata 12 Certified Master	TE0-147: Teradata 14 Comprehensive Mastery Exam

Exam Registration

All Teradata Certification exams are administered and proctored by authorized Prometric Testing Centers. Schedule exams at any authorized Prometric Testing Center by phone or online. In the US and Canada, you may call 1-877-887-6868. A listing of Prometric telephone numbers, by country, is available at:

www.prometric.com/Teradata. Some countries do not offer online registration.

Where to Find More Information

Teradata Corporation's official certification exams and credentials are developed, copyrighted, and managed solely by the Teradata Certified Professional Program (TCPP) team. There are no other Teradata authorized exams, certifications, or legitimate credentials in the IT industry. To achieve your training and certification goals, pursue only authorized processes and approved courses of study as outlined on the official TCPP Website: www.Teradata.com/Certification. A mobile app with access to all study guides, practice questions, and many more Teradata Certification and related resources is also available for a variety of devices. Please refer to the web site for additional information.

Chapter 2: Extended Logical Model

Certification Objectives

✓ Describe the inputs, outputs, and objectives for physical database design.

Before You Begin

You should be familiar with the following terms and concepts.

Terms	Key Concepts
Primary Key	Considerations for choosing a Primary Key
Foreign Key	Considerations for choosing a Foreign Key
Data Demographics	How to capture and utilize for analysis
ELDM	Explain how this assists in determining Primary and Secondary Indexes

Application Development Life Cycle

The development of a database and its applications involves many steps and people to be successful. There are people who will argue for a quick solution. That approach eventually costs more, displeases many, and doesn't help the company grow.

Here is an example of the steps of a development life cycle.

1. Business Discovery.
2. Logical Data Model (LDM).
3. Application Design.
4. Extended Logical Data Model (ELDM).
5. Physical Data Model (PDM).
6. Application Development.
7. Extract Transform Load (ETL/ELT).
8. Write Documentation/Productionize.
9. Assurance Testing.
10. Production Installation and Maintenance (return to 1-7 as needed). Continue on to 11.
11. Tuning and Capacity Planning (return to 1-7 as needed). Continue on to 12.
12. LDM/PDM Review (return to 1-7).

The process begins when a business need is identified. Then the data required to solve that need is identified through the process of creating a Logical Data Model. (Does the data currently exist within the company? Can it be derived from existing data? How will new data be captured?) The ATM (Activity Transaction Modeling) process covers steps 3, 4, and 5. Notice that Application Development comes after the Physical Model has been created. This ensures that the applications will take full advantage of the system and data architecture.

The goals of the Activity Transaction Modeling (ATM) process are as follows:

1. Define all domains and constraints.
2. Identify all applications.
3. Model application processing activities including their transactions and run frequencies.
4. Model each transaction using the following information:

   a. Identify tables used.
   b. Identify columns required for value and join access.
   c. Estimate qualifying cardinalities.
5. Summarize value and join access information across all transactions.
6. Add data demographics to the Table Access Summary by Columns report:
7. Table cardinalities.
8. Column value distributions (histograms).
9. Column change ratings.
10. End of process.

There are a series of suggested forms to document the findings of each step:

Action	ATM Form
Define all domains	Domains
Define all constraints	Constraints
Identify all applications in the system	System
Model each identified application	Application
Model each identified transaction	Report/Query Analysis
Summarize all value and join accesses	
Transfer access information	Table
Compile or estimate data demographics	
Identify column change ratings	

Figure 2.1

Logical Data Model

A logical model consists of the tables and columns of data needed to meet a business requirement. In some cases, existing tables may only need to be extended; in other cases new tables will be identified.

Here is an example of two relational tables that describe departments and employees. Including sample data helps make the model come alive and seem real. The sample data only has to be representative, not authoritative.

Department_Table

Dept_No	Department_Name	Mgr_Employee_No	Budget
PK	NN	FK	
200	Research and Development	1000234	550000.00
100	Marketing	1256349	500000.00
400	Customer Support	1256349	500000.00
300	Sales	1333454	650000.00
500	Human Resources	1121334	450000.00

Employee_Table

Employee_No	Dept_No	Mgr_Employee_No	Last_Name	First_Name	Salary
PK	FK	FK	NN	NN	
2000000	?	1121334	Travolta	John	32800.50
1333454	200	1121334	Roberts	Julia	48800.00
1000232	10	1121334	Gere	Richard	64300.00
1256349	400	1333454	Ford	Harrison	54590.00
1232578	100	1256349	Student	Mandee	48850.00
1121334	400	?	Strickland	Stan	54590.00
2341218	400	1256349	Clooney	George	35000.00
1324657	200	1000234	Willis	Bruce	42788.88
2312225	300	1333454	McFly	Loraine	40200.00

Figure 2.2

Primary Keys (PK)

There can only be one Primary Key per table, though there may be candidate keys that could serve the same purpose. The PK can also contain more than one column and Relational Theory states that there is no limit to the number of columns in a PK. Here are some additional characteristics regarding PK's.

- The PK uniquely identifies every row in a table (No Duplicates – ND).
- The PK cannot be null (No Nulls - NN).
- The PK cannot be changed (No Change – NC).
- The PK does not imply an access path.

Foreign Keys (FK)

An FK is a PK elsewhere in the model (same/different table) and there can be zero to many FKs in a table. Below are some additional characteristics of FK's.

- An FK can contain duplicate values, unless marked ND.
- An FK can be NULL, unless marked NN.
- An FK can be changed, unless marked NC.
- An FK does not imply an access path.

Here is a diagram showing the relationships created by the PKs/FKs from the relational tables illustrated in figure 2.2.

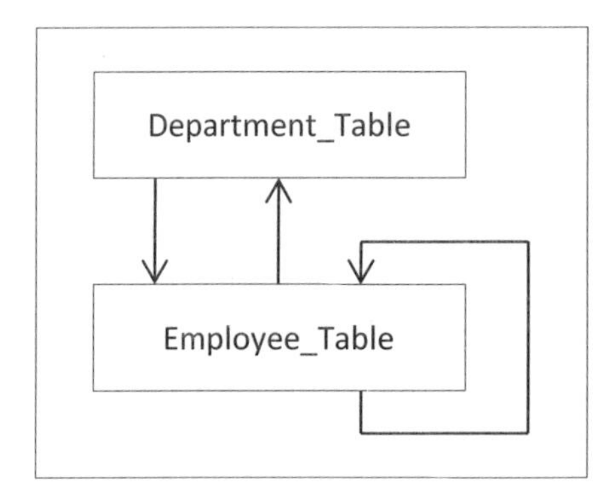

Figure 2.3

Normalization

Normalization is the typical process used for developing relational data models. All of the tables in a good Logical Data Model adhere to the three main rules of normalization.

First Normal Form (1NF)	Attributes must not repeat within a table No repeating groups Every attribute must have a 1:1 relationship to the PK
Second Normal Form (2NF)	Attributes must relate to the entire Primary Key, not just a portion of it Tables with a single-column PK (entities) are always in 2NF

Third Normal Form (3NF)	Attributes must relate only to the Primary Key and not to each other Cover up the PK and any No Duplicate (ND) columns and the remaining columns must not describe each other

Figure 2.4

Extended Logical Data Model (ELDM)

The LDM is complete after the users have signed off on it. The next step is to gather physical information about the data and add it to the mode to create the Extended Logical Data Model (ELDM), which is vital in designing the final Physical Data Model (PDM).

Column ACCESS in the WHERE Clause

The column names appearing in a WHERE clause will determine row values returned for display or processing (SELECT), updates (UPDATE) or deletes (DELETE) Therefore, demographics for those columns (single or multiple) become an important addition to the ELDM.

Data Demographics

In the majority of cases, data demographics can be gleaned from existing data, even if that data exists in non-relational form. Otherwise, interview the users and get their best guess. Use known maximums rather than averages. Systems based on averages fail when needed the most.

Demographics should be documented for all ACCESS columns, and Primary Key column sets. These values will help make intelligent physical design choices.

Distinct Values

If the data exists in a database, the number of unique values in the access column(s) can be determined by running the query shown in the following example.

```
SELECT COUNT(DISTINCT(column_name))
FROM    tablename;
```

Figure 2.5

Maximum Rows Per Value

The high row count for a non-null value can be determined by running the following query.

```
SELECT COUNT(*), column_name
FROM    table_name
WHERE column_name IS NOT NULL
GROUP BY column_name
ORDER BY 1 DESC;
```

Figure 2.6

This query's result set will also show the frequency distribution of all distinct values, and can be helpful in determining the next ATM parameter.

Typical Rows Per Value

This ATM parameter can be very subjective if there are large spikes in the distribution of values. As the parameter name implies, this counts the rows that the most frequently run WHERE clauses return. When in doubt, choose the highest value.

NULL Values

For each ACCESS column, you also need to know how many rows contain NULL values, and whether there are selects, updates, or deletes that search for them.

The following query will show how many rows contain nulls in the ACCESS column(s).

```
SELECT COUNT(*)
FROM   table_name
WHERE column_name IS NULL;
```

Figure 2.7

Change Rating

This is a relative measure (0 – 9) of how stable or volatile data values are.

CHANGE RATING	MEANING
0	The data in this column never changes Examples would be a person's birth date, or an employee's employee number PK column(s) should always have this change rating
1	Data in this column rarely changes An example would be a person's last name
2 through 8	User defined
9	The data is very volatile and changes frequently

Figure 2.8

ELDM Template

The following diagram shows the final form of the ATM process -- the **Table** form. This template summarizes all of the information from the other forms and will eventually include the final physical design decisions for Primary and Secondary Indexes. Any additional structures, such as Value Ordered Indexes, and Join Indexes should be documented on separate Table forms.

Table Page: ________ Of ________				ELDM Page: ________ System: ____________
Table Name		**Table Type**	**Cardinality**	**Data Protection**
Column Name				
PK/FK/ID				
Constraint Number				
Value Access Frequency				
Join Access Frequency				
Join Access Rows				
Distinct Values				
Maximum Rows/Value				
Maximum Rows/Null				
Typical Rows/Value				
Change Rating				
PI/SI				
Sample Data				

Figure 2.9

Chapter 2: Practice Questions

1. In the Logical Model, PK implies which of the following? (Choose 3)
    a. DD
    b. NN
    c. FK
    d. NC
    e. ND

2. Which Normal Form does the following table violate?

    Employee

emp_no	last_nm	first_nm	job_code	hire_dt	job_desc
PK					

    a. 1NF
    b. 2NF
    c. 3NF

3. The ________ is complete after the users have signed off on it. A next step is to gather physical information about the data and add it to the __________ to create the ________________, which is vital in designing the _____________.
    a. ELDM, ELDM, PDM, LDM
    b. LDM, ELDM, ELDM, PDM
    c. LDM, LDM, ELDM, PDM
    d. PDM, LDM, ELDM, LDM

4. Put the following development steps in their proper order.
    a. __ Application Development.
    b. __ Physical Data Model (PDM).
    c. __ Logical Data Model (LDM).
    d. __ Extended Logical Data Model (ELDM).
    e. __ Business Discovery.

5. Which Normal Form does the following table violate?

Sales_History

	Monthly_Sales_Amount					
sales_emp_no	M_1	M_2	M_3	M_4	M_5	M_6
PK						

    a. 1NF
    b. 2NF
    c. 3NF

Chapter Notes

Utilize this space for notes, key points to remember, diagrams, areas of further study, etc.

Chapter 3: Physical Data Model (PDM)

Certification Objectives

- ✓ Explain the effect of the Primary Index choices on physical design.

Before You Begin

You should be familiar with the following terms and concepts.

Terms	Key Concepts
Primary Indexes	How does the Primary Key impact the Primary Index choice
Secondary Indexes	What are the factors and impacts on the physical design
Join Frequency	Considerations for choosing the Primary Index
NUSI	How to calculate a strongly versus weakly selective NUSI

Primary and Secondary Index Factors

The following list of factors illustrates the complexity of Teradata Database index selection. It's important to follow the ATM process to make the optimal choices.

1. Nonspecific Factors
    - Degree of normalization of the database
    - How the Optimizer might use the index
    - Table type indexed
        - Major entity
        - Minor entity
        - Sub-entity

2. Primary index partitioning type
    - Non-partitioned
    - Partitioned
        - Single-level
        - Multilevel

3. Space utilization factors
    - How much space does the index occupy?
    - Type of data protection specified

4. Demographic factors
    - Cardinality of the table
    - Number of distinct column values
    - Maximum rows per value
    - Columns most frequently used to access table rows
    - Are rows most commonly accessed by values or by a join?
    - Degree of skew of column values

5. Application factors - In which application environment are rows most commonly accessed?

- Decision support
- OLTP
- Event queues
- Tactical queries
- Ad hoc queries
- Range queries
- Batch reporting
- Batch maintenance

6. Transaction factors
   - How are transactions written?
   - How are transactions parceled?
   - What levels and types of locking does a transaction require?
   - How long does the transaction hold locks?

7. DML Factors
   - Number of DELETE operations and when they occur
   - Number of INSERT operations and when they occur
   - Number of UPDATE operations and when they occur

System Generated Keys

Every relational table must have a Primary Key which serves to uniquely identify every row in a table. The Primary Key for entities should be the following:

1. A single column
2. Non-decomposable
3. A numeric value

If an entity table does not have a column satisfying those criteria, then an alternative is to have the system generate a Primary Key value (PK, SA).

Natural Key

A Natural Key is any real-world identifier that can be used as a unique identifier. An example would be employee numbers assigned to employees, codes used to represent specific conditions or events, and credit/debit card numbers.

Surrogate Key

A Surrogate Key is a system-generated simple numeric key. Often used when a natural key is otherwise difficult or impossible to define for a table or when the situation demands a non-composite primary key, but no natural non-composite exists.

Step 1 - Review Distribution

For all columns used for access (Value or Join). A histogram of the distribution of values can be helpful. Any column(s) with an uneven distribution will require additional study for their suitability as an index. The following bar chart depicts uneven distribution.

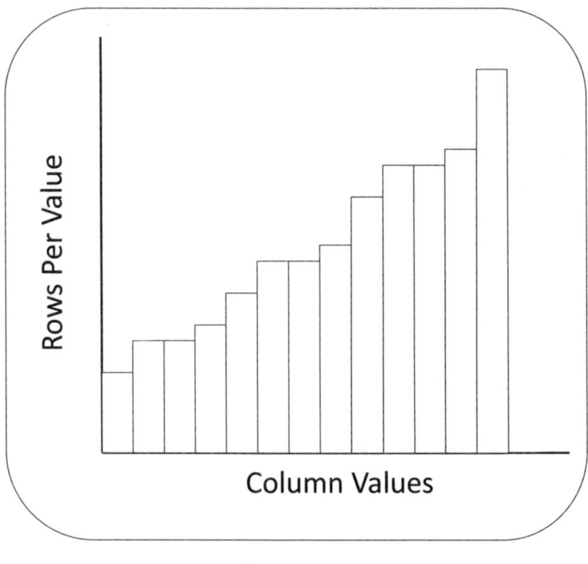

Figure 3.1

Step 2 - Eliminate based on Change Rating

Column(s) that have a change rating greater than 0 are poor choices for a Primary Index. Column(s) with a change rating greater than 2 are poor choices for Secondary Indexes. There is a great deal of overhead involved whenever an indexed column value changes. This will become apparent in coming modules.

Step 3 - NUSI Elimination via Value Access Frequency

Using the ATM Application form, eliminate those columns having a low access frequency. Although users may want "instant" response times for a DSS query, the Teradata architecture makes doing full-table scans very efficient.

Step 4 - Choose the Primary Index

Frequently, the Primary Key of a table is chosen for a Unique Primary Index (UPI), which guarantees smooth, even distribution across all of the AMPs. Smooth distribution of table rows is essential to providing good service levels to all users.

In some cases, a Non-Unique Primary Index (NUPI) can be chosen to cause the table rows to be stored on the same AMPs as the table rows to which they are frequently joined.

Step 5 - Choose the Secondary Indexes

Any Candidate Key (No Duplicates, Not Null) can be a candidate for a Unique Secondary Index (USI). Other columns marked ND (No Duplicates) are also USI candidates. A USI will allow one row with a NULL value. A USI can also be used to enforce uniqueness for the Primary Key when a NUPI is chosen for a table.

Note: Choose NUSIs for those columns having a high access frequency, low change rating, and that are strongly selective.

Join Access Frequency Priority

The Application form identifies the known or expected, joins. Use it to rank the joins. Those that occur frequently may be accommodated by the judicious selection of UPIs and NUPIs. Others may be better served through the creation of a Join Index. Those that occur infrequently should probably be left to standard join processing.

Note: Secondary indexes (USI, NUSI) are only considered by the Parser for Nested joins.

Value Access Frequency Priority

Use the Application form to also rank the value accesses. Keep in mind that there are search conditions which typically invoke a full-table scan of the base table or of a secondary index subtable when used as a HAVING or WHERE clause condition because they do not specify a specific value or set of values.

USI to Eliminate Duplicate Row Checking

When a row is inserted into a Set table having a NUPI, the system must do a row-by-row check of every table row having the same row hash as the new row to ensure the new row will not create a duplicate row. If the NUPI is strongly selective (few rows per row hash), the duplicate row check is very quick, since all of the rows are most likely in the same data block. The more weakly selective the NUPI, the longer the checking takes. It could also require additional data block I/Os. Creating a USI on the table allows the system to do a duplicate index value check, eliminating the row-by-row checking of the base table rows.

NUSI Considerations

Creating a NUSI doesn't mean the Parser will consider using it unless it's less expensive than doing a full-table scan. The only way to know whether a NUSI will be used is to create it. If the Parser ignores the NUSI -- drop it.

Multi-Column NUSI Columns Used as a Covered Query

If a NUSI is based on all of the columns needed to satisfy a query, the Optimizer can use the index by itself and will never need to access the base table rows. This is an example of vertical partitioning.

Value-Ordered NUSIs

Normally, index rows of a NUSI are stored in row hash order. For that reason, queries doing a range check will default to a full-table scan. An option exists that will store the index rows in order of their data value, making queries over a range of values using the NUSI possible.

Note: Remember to collect statistics on all of your indexes and to verify with an EXPLAIN.

A Formula for Calculating a Strongly Selective NUSI

A strongly selective NUSI is one that accesses less than one row per data block.

Strongly selective NUSI = Rows/Value < Data Blocks/AMP

A weakly selective NUSI accesses one or more rows per data block. If all of the data blocks would have to be accessed, the Parser will ignore the NUSI (and its processing overhead) and perform a full-table scan.

Weakly selective NUSI = Rows/Value >= 1 Data Block/AMP

Typical Row and Block Sizes

There are two Row Size forms that can be used to calculate the size of a table's rows. One form is for 32-bit systems, and the other is for 64-bit systems. Even though the forms take the number of variable length and compressed columns into consideration, the actual affected rows can vary. Therefore, the row size calculation should serve as the typical row size. Keep in mind that rows must be an even number of bytes in length.

Just as rows vary in size, so can data blocks. Blocks vary in size from 1 to 255 sectors. In 32-bit systems, a sector is 512 bytes. In 64-bit systems, a sector is 1024 bytes.

As rows grow and shrink through updates, and as rows are inserted and deleted, block splits will occur. The following formula can be used to determine the typical multi-row block size.

Typical Block Size = $\frac{\text{Max Block Size}}{2}$ + 1 additional Sector (in bytes)

Chapter 3: Practice Questions

1. What Change Rating is best for PI column candidates?
    a. 0
    b. 1
    c. 2
    d. 3-8
    e. 9

2. Given the following table definition and insert statements, how many of the inserts will succeed?

    create table t1(c1 smallint, c2 smallint)
    unique primary index (c1);

    insert into t1 values(null, 3);
    insert into t1 values(5, 7);
    insert into t1 values(null, 5);
    insert into t1 values(5, 3);

    a. 1
    b. 2
    c. 3
    d. 4

3. What is the disk sector size in 64-bit systems?
    a. 128
    b. 256
    c. 512
    d. 1024
    e. 2048

4. Given the following table definition and insert statements, how many of the inserts will fail?

```
create table t2(c1 int, c2 int, c3 int) primary index(c1)
unique index(c2, c3);

insert into t2 values(1, 2, 3);
insert into t2 values(1,  , 3);
insert into t2 values(1, 2,  );
insert into t2 values(1,  ,  );
insert into t2 values(1,  , 2);
insert into t2 values(1, 3,  );
insert into t2 values(1, null, null);
```

   a. 0
   b. 1
   c. 2
   d. 3
   e. 4

5. Which of the following can be used to eliminate the duplicate row checking for any Set table having a weakly selective NUPI?
   a. A Value Ordered NUSI
   b. A covering NUSI
   c. A USI
   d. A join index
   e. A MLPPI

Chapter Notes

Utilize this space for notes, key points to remember, diagrams, areas of further study, etc.

Chapter 4: Data Distribution

Certification Objectives

- ✓ Given a scenario, identify when to use a NUPI.
- ✓ Given a scenario, identify when to use a UPI.
- ✓ Given a scenario, identify when to use a NoPI.

Before You Begin

You should be familiar with the following terms and concepts.

Terms	Key Concepts
Primary Index	Considerations for choosing a Primary Index
UPI	How does a UPI affect the distribution of a table
RowID	What is a RowID and how is it created
Access Methods	Understand the difference between accessing data via a UPI versus a NUPI

Primary Index

All Teradata Database tables require a primary index because the system distributes table rows to the AMPs based on their primary index values.

Primary Indexes can be either Unique (UPI) or Non-Unique (NUPI). Furthermore, they can be partitioned (PPI) or non-partitioned (NPPI). We will review Partitioned Primary Indexes in the next chapter.

Unique Primary Index (UPI)

As the name implies, a UPI will only allow one row per value. This can include one row that has a NULL value. The system is designed to provide even distribution of table rows as long as there are multiple rows per AMP.

Even with very large tables, the number of collisions (different data values hashing to the same AMP) is minimal.

Non-Unique Primary Index (NUPI)

The system will allow multiple rows to have the same Primary Index value, and will store them on the same AMP. These are duplicate index values, not collisions.

Though multiple rows can have the same index value, if the table is a SET table, the remaining columns must be at least one binary bit different from each other (no duplicate rows). If the table is MULTISET, a row is stored even if it is a duplicate of an existing row.

Primary Index and the Row Hash

When a row is INSERTed into a table, the value(s) for the Primary Index are fed into a hashing algorithm. The output of the hashing algorithm is a 32-bit row hash.

The Teradata Database hashing algorithm operates on the bit patterns of the data, not its external value. For example, a numeric value stored as a DECIMAL number with one precision produces a different hash code than the same numeric value stored as a DECIMAL value with a different precision. Additionally, a number typed as an integer requires only 4 bytes of storage, while its decimal representation might take as many as 8 bytes, depending on the size of the number.

Row Hash, Hash Map, and Hash Buckets

Instead of hashing to a location on disk, The Row Hash is used to identify an entry in a memory-resident Hash Map called a Hash Bucket. The BYNET maintains a copy of the Hash Map on every node.

A Teradata system Hash Map will either have 65,536 hash buckets, or 1,048,576 hash buckets. Each Hash Bucket points to a single AMP in the system, and multiple Hash Buckets will point to the same AMP. The upper portion (either 16 or 20 bits) of the Row Hash is used to identify a specific Hash Bucket. The BYNET directs rows to their proper AMP based upon the AMP number in the selected Hash Bucket.

Review: Inserting a Row on an AMP

- The Parser hashes the Primary Index value(s).
- The Parser gives the new row to the BYNET.
- The BYNET sends the row to the AMP assigned to the Hash Bucket identified by THE upper portion of the row hash.
- The AMP builds the physical row.
- Using the Master Index and Cylinder Index structures, the AMP accesses the data block for this TableID & Row Hash.
- The AMP then scans through the data block, in Row ID (Row Hash + Uniqueness Value) order, looking for the logical point of insertion.
    - If this is the first row with this Row Hash to be stored in this table, it is inserted into the data block with a Uniqueness Value of one.
- If the AMP encounters existing rows with the same Row Hash, they are either collisions, or NUPI duplicates.
    - If the index is unique (UPI), the system compares the index values to insure this is a collision rather than a duplicate index violation. It continues scanning to find the current highest Uniqueness Value assigned to rows

with this Row Hash, then increments that value by one to create the Uniqueness Value for the new row and stores the row.

- If the table is MULTISET, it skips over the collisions (no index value comparisons) to get the Uniqueness Value of the last row. It then increments that value by one to create the Uniqueness Value for the new row and stores the row.
- If the index is non-unique (NUPI), the AMP does a duplicate row check by comparing all of the new row's data against the existing row's data. If no duplicate row violation occurs, the AMP increments the Uniqueness Value of the last row by one and uses that value as the Uniqueness Value for the new row. It then stores the new row.

Unique Row Identifier

Though a 32-bit Row Hash allows for 4.2 billion values, there is always a chance of different input values generating the same Row Hash value. These are known as collisions.

Every table has its own set of data blocks. Rows of different tables never appear in the same data block. This minimizes the occurrence of collisions to a trivial level, but does not reduce NUPI duplicates.

In order to uniquely identify every row in a table, the system appends a 32-bit counter, called the Uniqueness Value, to the Row Hash. The first row in a table with a specific Row Hash is assigned a Uniqueness Value of one. The system increments the uniqueness value by one for each successive table row having the same Row Hash.

RowID for Unique Primary Index

The RowID for a UPI will either be 64 or 80 bits, depending on whether the index is partitioned.

The following diagram shows the RowID layout for both Non-Partitioned Primary Indexes (NPPI) and Partitioned Primary Indexes (PPI) with two-byte partitioning. Partitioned Primary Indexes are discussed in the next chapter. Unless there is a hash collision, every row will have a Uniqueness Value of 1.

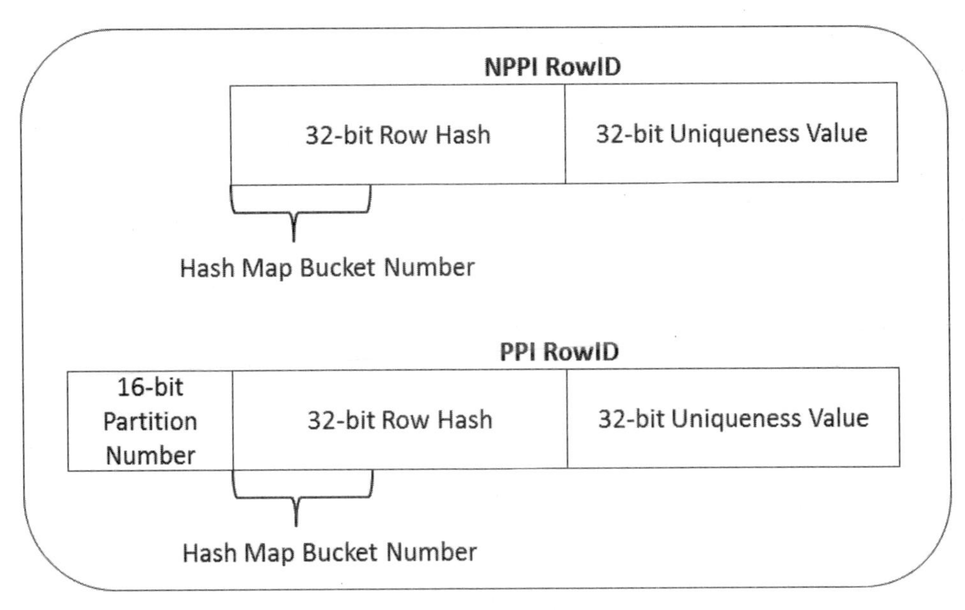

Figure 4.1

RowID for Non-Unique Primary Index

The RowID for a NUPI is exactly the same as a UPI. The difference is the index values do not have to be unique. Multiple rows could have the same Row Hash value, but each will have a different Uniqueness Value.

Row Retrieval Using the Primary Index

The following diagram shows how the system goes about finding and storing a NPPI row based upon its Primary Index.

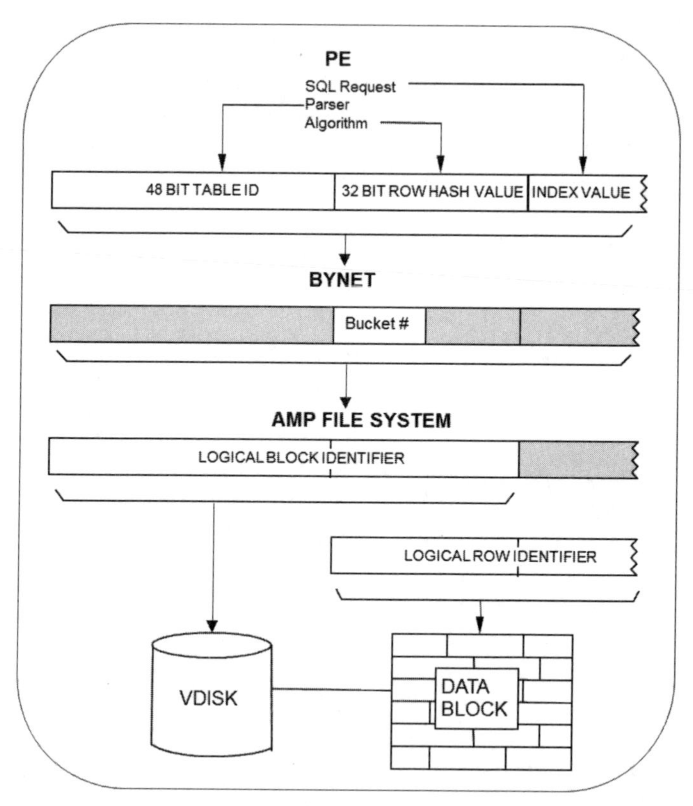

Figure 4.2

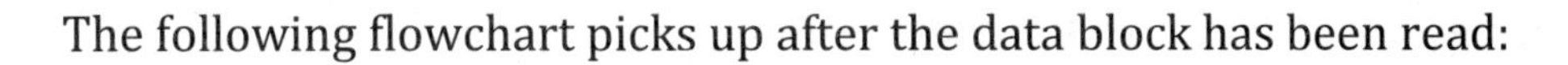

The following flowchart picks up after the data block has been read:

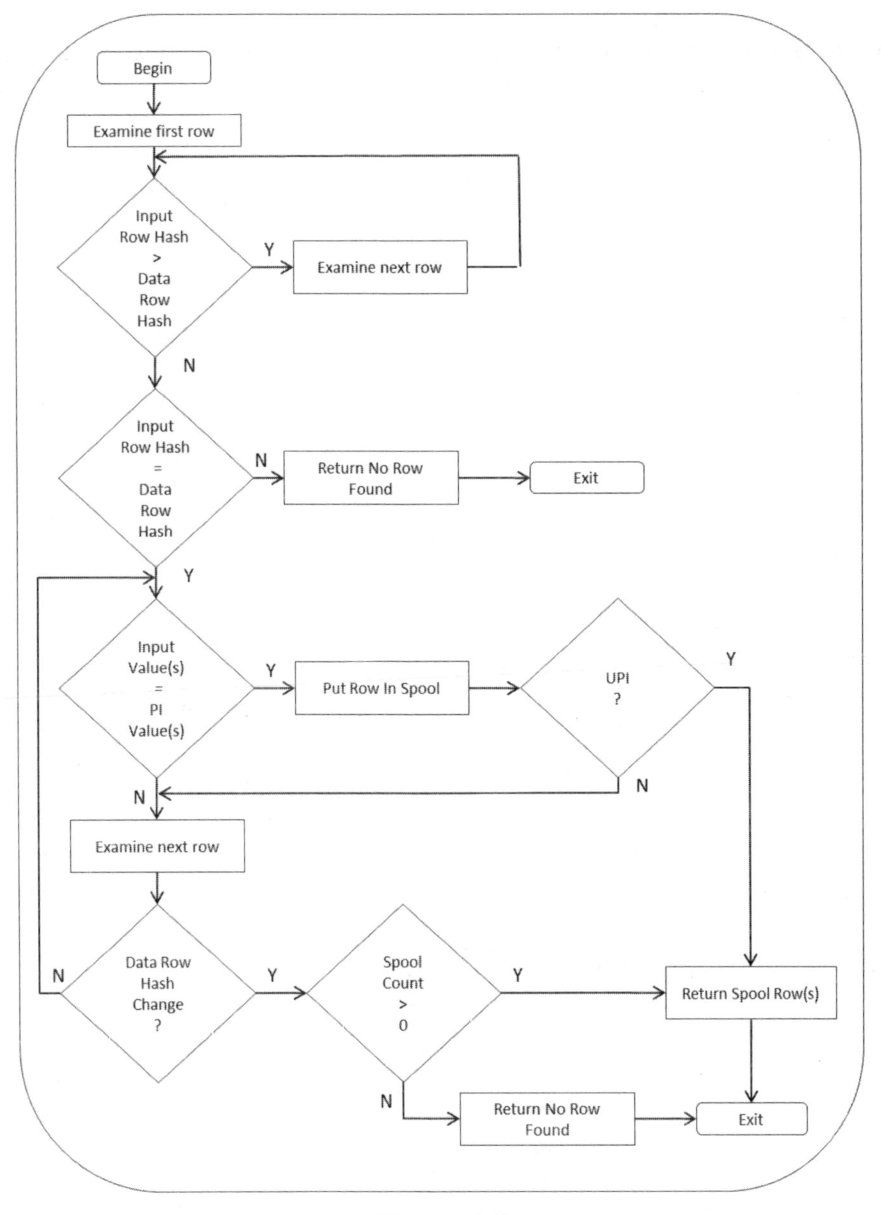

Figure 4.3

Checking for Collisions

Collisions occur when different index values in a table generate the same Row Hash. That is why the index value(s) are included in the retrieval message sent by the PE to the AMP. By comparing the search index value(s) against existing index value(s) of rows with the same Row Hash, the system can differentiate between collisions and matches.

Row Distribution - NUPIs

The system attempts to keep NUPI duplicates in the same data block to minimize I/O. Very large rows or a high number of rows per value may cause NUPI duplicates to be stored on multiple data blocks. The impact is increased I/O to store and retrieve the data blocks.

Row Distribution - UPIs

There are 1,048,576 buckets in the Hash Map. These are spread as evenly as possible across all of the AMPs. The upper 20 bits of the Row Hash identify one bucket, which in turn identifies the AMP that owns that Row Hash.

Keep in mind that the same data value, stored in the same data type, will produce the same Row Hash. Employee #100 (INT), Department #100 (INT) and Part #100 (INT) will all hash to the same AMP, but will be stored in separate data blocks.

How Teradata Handles Data Distribution

The massively parallel architecture of the Teradata system has a data distribution method that is fast and flexible with no need to constantly reorganize pointers for efficiency. That method is called hashing.

A Hash Code derived from the Primary Index randomizes a row to a specific AMP, not a physical location on disk. Using the Row Hash, the AMP file system zeroes in on the data block, a table row where that Hash Code belongs, and either stores or retrieves the row(s).

NoPI (No Primary Index)

A NoPI table is a MULTISET nontemporal table that does not have a primary index. The chief purpose of NoPI tables is to enhance the performance of FastLoad and Teradata Parallel Data Pump Array INSERT data loading operations.

Because there is no primary index for the rows of a NoPI table, its rows are not hashed to an AMP based on their primary index value. Instead, Teradata Database either hashes on the Query ID for a row, or it uses a different algorithm to assign the row to its home AMP. Once a row reaches the AMP onto which it has been FastLoaded, Teradata Database generates a RowID for each row in the NoPI table by randomly selecting an arbitrary hash bucket that the AMP owns and uses it to generate a RowID. This strategy makes fallback and index maintenance very similar to their maintenance on a PI table.

Note: Both global temporary tables and volatile tables can be defined as NoPI tables, but temporal tables cannot.

FastLoad can load Primary Index (PI) tables defined as MULTISET, but all duplicate rows are discarded. The target table is treated as if it were a SET table. NoPI tables must be MULTISET, but no duplicate row checking is possible (duplicate rows can be on different AMPs). Therefore, when FastLoad targets a NoPI table, duplicate row checking is disabled.

Row Hash Value and RowID Assignment

When a table has a Primary Index, the Primary Index values are passed to the Hashing Algorithm, which then produces a 32-bit row hash. This is shown in the following diagram

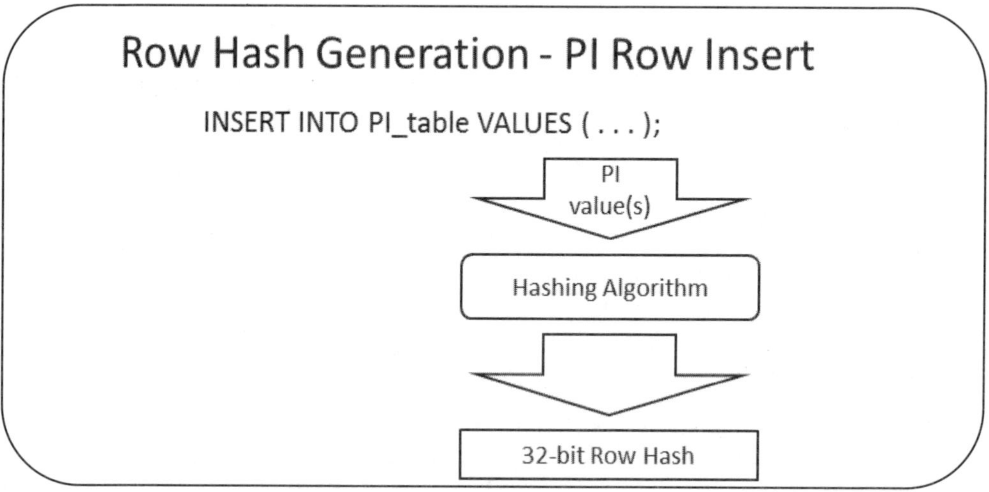

Figure 4.4

Because NoPI tables have no primary index on which to base the row hash value for a row, the Teradata Database generates a random row hash value for NoPI table rows based on different values. These row hash values are generated differently depending on whether the row is inserted using an SQL ARRAY insert operation via Teradata Parallel Data Pump, or loaded using FastLoad.

For simple SQL insert operations, Teradata Database uses the system-generated value of the Query ID to uniquely identify requests as input to the hashing algorithm to determine its destination AMP. This is shown in the following diagram.

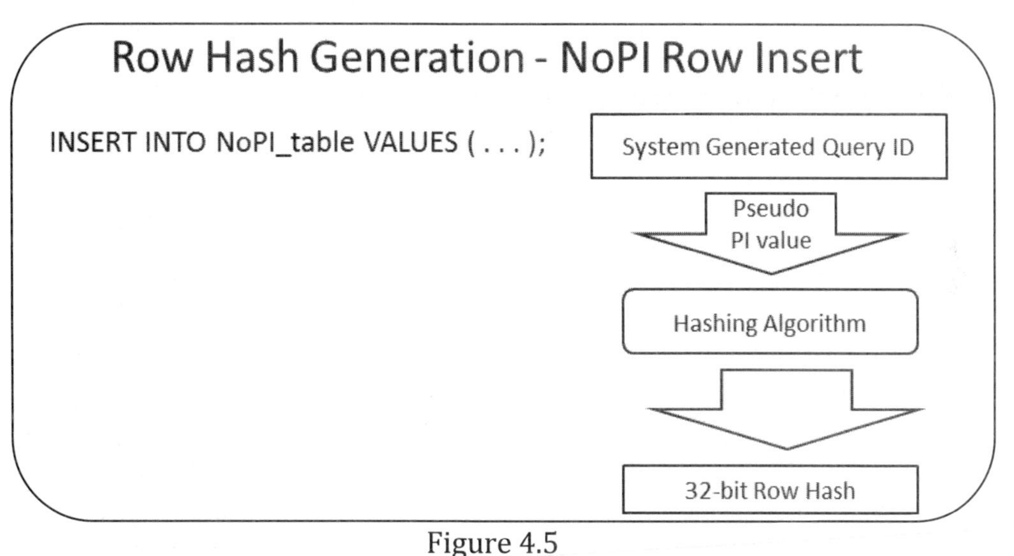

Figure 4.5

The Query ID uses the PE vproc ID in its high digits and a counter-based value in its low digits, which supports both single-session and multiple-sessions INSERT operations equally well. The row hash value generated by the hashing algorithm ensures that rows are ordinarily sent to a different AMP from the AMP selected for the previous request, which balances the distribution of rows among the AMPs as much as is possible without hashing on a primary index value. The randomly generated hash bucket values are as nonunique as possible to avoid excessive skewing of the row distribution.

For simple insert operations, there are two possible cases:

- A single row is to be dispatched.
    - This is the case for a standard INSERT operation.
- Multiple rows are to be dispatched.

- This is the case for the Array INSERT operations used by the Teradata Parallel Data Pump utility.

For both cases, the system copies the generated row hash value into the RowID of each row. Since the system uses the generated row hash value only once per request, Teradata Database copies the same row hash value into the RowID of *all* the rows processed by an Array INSERT operation, which means they are all sent to the same AMP, very possibly in the same step.

The source spool for rows that are inserted into NoPI tables by INSERT...SELECT operations are simply appended on an AMP-local basis to their target table. There is no need to hash them to a destination AMP since they're already there.

Rows loaded using FastLoad sends rows to its AMP during acquisition from client blocks and then directly to target AMPs in round-robin fashion. Each target AMP then uses its lowest hash bucket assignment as the row hash for the block's rows, with the remaining 48-bit or 44-bit serving as uniqueness values which, together, form rowids for the rows.

Teradata Database uses a 44-bit RowID Uniqueness Value, so there can be approximately 17 x 10^{12} rows per hash bucket per AMP. NoPI table rows always begin with a Uniqueness Value of 1, and as more rows are inserted into the table, their Uniqueness Values are incremented sequentially.

Uses

NoPI tables are particularly useful as staging tables for bulk data loads. When a table has no primary index, its rows can be dispatched to any arbitrary AMP. This allows the system to load data into a staging table faster and more. By storing bulk loaded rows on any arbitrary AMP, the performance impact for both CPU and I/O is reduced significantly. Once loaded, all of the rows can be appended to a NoPI table without being checked for duplicates or needing to be redistributed to their hash-owning AMPs. Also, there is no requirement for NoPI tables to maintain their rows in any particular order, so the system doesn't sort them.

The performance advantage realized from NoPI tables is achieved for applications that typically load data into a primary-indexed staging table, which must first undergo a conversion to some other form, and then be *re*distributed before they are stored in a second table.

Another advantage of NoPI tables is that you can be finished with the acquisition phase of the utility operation sooner, which frees client resources for other applications. NoPI tables can serve as staging tables for temporal tables, though temporal tables cannot be NoPI tables.

You can also use NoPI tables as a sandbox tables when an appropriate primary index has not yet been defined for the primary-indexed table they will eventually populate. This enables you to experiment with several different primary index possibilities before deciding on the most optimal choice for your particular application workloads.

Access Methods

The following summarizes the various access methods, the number of AMPs involved, and the number of rows returned.

ACCESS METHOD	NUMBER OF AMPs	ROWS RETURNED
UPI	1	0 OR 1
NUPI	1	0, 1, OR MORE
USI	2	0 OR 1
NUSI	ALL	0, 1, OR MORE
FULL TABLE SCAN	ALL	0, 1, TO ALL

Figure 4.6

Chapter 4: Practice Questions

1. How many hash buckets can the Hash Maps can be configured for? (Choose 2)
    a. 32.768
    b. 65,536
    c. 131,072
    d. 262,144
    e. 1,048,576

2. How many bits from the upper portion of a Row Hash will the system use to identify a specific Hash Map Bucket? (Choose 2)
    a. 12
    b. 14
    c. 16
    d. 18
    e. 20

3. For each Access Method, choose the correct Number of AMPs and Rows Returned.

	Access Method		
a	Full Table Scan		
b	UPI		
c	NUSI		
d	USI		
e	NUPI		

	# of AMPs
f	1
g	2
h	ALL

	Rows Returned
i	0, 1, OR ALL
j	0 OR 1
k	0, 1, OR MORE

4. NoPI table's main advantage is in support of _______ applications.
    a. Business
    b. ELT
    c. ETL
    d. OLTP

5. On a standard row INSERT into a NoPI table, the RowId is assigned by the _____.
    a. PE
    b. BYNET
    c. AMP
    d. DSU

Chapter Notes

Utilize this space for notes, key points to remember, diagrams, areas of further study, etc.

Chapter 5: Partitioned Primary Indexes

Certification Objectives

- ✓ Describe how to construct the partitioning expression for a PPI table.
- ✓ Given a scenario, describe the effects of altering a partitioning expression.
- ✓ Given a scenario, describe the effects of using the ALTER TABLE TO CURRENT.
- ✓ Given a scenario, determine when it is appropriate to ALTER a table vs. CREATE a new PPI or NPPI table.
- ✓ Given a scenario, identify when to use a Character PPI.
- ✓ Given a scenario, identify when to use a MLPPI.
- ✓ Given a scenario, identify when to use a PPI.
- ✓ Given a scenario, identify when to use Column Partitioning (CP).
- ✓ Given a scenario, identify when to use the NO AUTO compress option for Column Partitioning.
- ✓ Identify issues to consider when using NO RANGE on PPI tables.

Before You Begin

You should be familiar with the following terms and concepts.

Terms	Key Concepts
PPI	Considerations for choosing a Partitioned Primary Index versus a NPPI
MLPPI	Understanding the performance impact and options available
Alter Table	How this work on a PPI table

No Range	When to utilize and best practices
Column Partitioning	The difference between column and row partitioning

Primary Index Access (NPPI)

Rows of a table are stored in RowID order within their data blocks. They are retrieved by their Row Hash and Index value. Refer back to Figure 4.1 and 4.2.

Partitioned Primary Index (PPI) Access

If a table has a Partitioned Primary Index, the system adds two or eight more bytes to each row to identify its partition (see Figure 4.1). PPI rows are sorted and stored in RowID order within their Partition Number. They are retrieved by Partition Number, Row Hash, and Index value.

Implementing PPI

Partitioning of a table can be accomplished through the CREATE TABLE or ALTER TABLE commands.

You can define both single-level and multilevel PPIs for global temporary and volatile tables, for standard base tables (but not queue tables), and for non-compressed join indexes.

When a table or join index is created with a PPI, its rows are hashed to the appropriate AMPs and then assigned to their computed internal partition number based on the value of a partitioning expression defined by the user when the table was created or altered. Once assigned to a partition, the rows are stored in row hash order.

The partitioning columns do not have to be part of a NUPI, but they must be part of a UPI. If the table has a UPI, consider changing to a NUPI and adding a USI to enforce uniqueness instead.

Note: With TD14, there can be up to 2^{62} (approximately 9.2 quintillion - BIGINT) partitions. If the number determined by the partitioning expression can fit into 2^{15} (65,535 - SMALLINT) partitions, then it uses a 2-byte partition number, else it uses an 8-byte partition number.

Partition Elimination and Full Table Scans

On a NPPI table, if a SELECT request does not specify the values for all the primary index columns, an all-AMP full-table scan will be done if there is no usable secondary index. However, with a PPI, if conditions are specified on the partitioning columns, partition elimination might reduce what would otherwise be an all-AMP full-table scan to an all-AMP scan of only the partitions that are not eliminated. The extent of partition elimination depends on the partitioning expressions, the conditions specified in the query, and the ability of the Optimizer to recognize such opportunities.

Accessing via the Primary Index in a PPI Table

If a SELECT request specifies values for all the primary index columns, the AMP that contains those rows can be determined and only one AMP needs to be accessed. If the query conditions are not specified on the partitioning columns, then each partition can be probed to find the rows based on the hash value, assuming there is no usable alternative index. If conditions are also specified on the partitioning columns, then partition elimination might further reduce the number of partitions to be probed on that AMP.

Accessing via the Primary Index on PPI Table Workaround

A well-constructed PPI table with proper coding will be a one AMP and a one I/O operation. The worst-case scenario occurs when a query utilizes the PI column that is not part of the partitioning column set. In this situation, you will see an all partition scan on a single AMP in order to find the appropriate PI value. In addition, the number of disk reads could increase to equal the number of partitions on the PPI table. Even though this is a fast operation, a table with thousands of partitions could prove to be problematic for applications that require true PI performance.

One solution is to define a unique secondary index (USI) on the same column(s) as the primary index. This approach is not as fast as accessing the non-Partitioned Primary Index column, since a USI access is always a two AMP and two I/O operation. However, a USI is independent of the number of partitions in the table and should provide good performance for applications.

The second option is to ensure that users include the PI and PPI columns in their queries.

Partitioning with CASE_N

Building a partitioning expression on CASE_N or other functions and expressions is a reasonable thing to do if *all* the following items are true:

- The partitioning expression defines a mapping between conditions and INTEGER numbers.
- The partitioning expression is not based on a DATE column.
- Your query workloads against the table use equality conditions on the partitioning columns to specify a single partition.

- You have no need to alter the partitioning of the table
- You get the plans and data maintenance you need

Note: The default Optimizer assumption of 65,535 partitions provides good query plans. This does not apply to CASE_N unless the function is embedded within a larger partitioning expression.

The following is an example of CASE_N partitioning:

```
CREATE TABLE Order_Table ...
PRIMARY INDEX (customer_number)
PARTITION BY CASE_N (Order_Total < 1000,      -- 1st partition
                     Order_Total < 10000,     -- 2nd partition
                     Order_Total < 100000);   -- 3rd partition
```

Figure 5.1

RANGE_N Partitioning

The RANGE_N function is provided to simplify the specification of common partitioning expressions where each partition contains a range of data. It is especially useful when the column contains a date.

```
CREATE TABLE Order_Table ...
PRIMARY INDEX (Customer_Number)
PARTITION BY RANGE_N
      (Order_Date BETWEEN DATE '2001-01-01'
       AND DATE '2011-12-31'     /* 132 partitions defined based */
      EACH INTERVAL '1' MONTH);     /* (1) month intervals */
```

Figure 5.2

PPI with Multiple Ranges Defined

You can specify multiple ranges for a partitioning expression. The following is an example:

```
CREATE TABLE . . .
PRIMARY INDEX (x)
PARTITION BY RANGE_N
( y BETWEEN 1 AND 100, 101 AND 300, 301 AND 500);
```

Figure 5.3

CHARACTER PPI

Though partitioning frequently uses numeric or date columns, partitioning on character data can be done. A typical example would be to partition addresses by their two character state code.

Care must be taken in choosing whether to use CASE_N or RANGE_N partitioning.

CHARACTER CASE_N

Using CASE_N allows you to define specific state code matches. The following example creates 5 partitions.

```
PARTITION BY (CASE_N(state_code = 'HI', state_code = 'PR',
state_code = 'VI', NO CASE, UNKNOWN))
```

In this example, Hawaii addresses go to partition 1, Puerto Rico addresses go to partition 2, Virgin Islands addresses go to partition 3, all other two-character combinations go to partition 4, and null state codes go to partition 5.

The next example creates three partitions.

```
PARTITION BY (CASE_N(state_code IN('HI', 'PR', 'VI'), NO CASE,
UNKNOWN))
```

In this example, addresses for Hawaii, Puerto Rico, and the Virgin Islands go to partition 1, all other two-character combinations go to partition 2, and nulls go to partition 3.

CHARACTER RANGE_N

In choosing RANGE_N for character partitioning, the test values must appear in ascending collation mode sequence. The following examples assume ASCII collation mode.

This example changes the first CASE_N into a RANGE_N partitioning expression.

```
PARTITION BY (RANGE_N (state_code BETWEEN 'HI', 'PR', 'VI'
AND 'ZZ', NO RANGE, UNKNOWN))
```

Once again, the system creates 5 partitions. However, there is a big difference where two-character values other than 'HI', 'PR', and 'VI' go.

Two-character values equal to or greater than 'HI' and less than 'PR' go to partition 1. Two-character values equal to or greater than 'PR' and less than 'VI' go to partition 2. Two-character values equal to or greater than 'VI' and less than 'ZZ' go to partition 3, Two-character values less than 'HI' or greater than or equal to 'ZZ' go to partition 4, and nulls go to partition 5.

You can also use an asterisk (*) to specify the starting expression and/or the ending expression. Here's an example.

```
PARTITION BY (RANGE_N( state_code BETWEEN * AND 'HI',
'PR', 'VI' AND *, UNKNOWN))
```

This example creates five partitions. All two-character values less than 'HI' go into partition 1. Partition 2 contains two-character values equal to or greater than 'HI' and less than 'PR'. Partition 3 contains all two-character values equal to or greater than 'PR' and less than 'VI'. Partition 4 contains all two-character values equal to or greater than 'VI', and partition 5 contains any null values.

Implementing Multi-Level Partitioned Primary Indexes

Multilevel partitioning allows each partition at a given level to be further partitioned into sub-partitions. Each partition for a level is sub-partitioned the same per a partitioning expression defined for the next lower level. The system hash orders the rows within the lowest partition levels. A multilevel PPI (MLPPI) undertakes efficient searches by using partition elimination at the various levels or combinations of levels.

Note: For a Multi-level Partitioned Primary Indexes - 2-byte partitioning expression. When using an "ADD" clause, it will keep any subsequent ALTER statements from exceeding this partition number size, thus keeping it to under 8 bytes. This is because you are not allowed to ALTER the partition expression to move from a 2-byte number to an 8-byte number.

Figure 5.4 is an example of creating a table with three levels of partitioning out of the maximum of 15:

```
CREATE TABLE part_x
(c1 BYTEINT
,c2 BYTEINT
,c3 BYTEINT
,c4 BYTEINT)
PRIMARY INDEX (c1, c2, c3)
PARTITION BY (RANGE_N(c1 BETWEEN 1 AND 2 EACH 1)
             ,RANGE_N(c2 BETWEEN 1 AND 2 EACH 1)
             ,RANGE_N(c3 BETWEEN 1 AND 2 EACH 1));
```

Figure 5.4

The first partitioning expression (c1) is the highest level. Within each of those partitions, the second partitioning expression (c2) defines how each of the c1 partitions is sub-partitioned. Within each of those c2 partitions, the third-level partitioning expression (c3) defines how each of the c2 partitions is sub-partitioned. Within each of these lowest level (c3) partitions, rows are ordered by the row hash value of their primary index and their assigned uniqueness value.

MLPPI Examples

The next example modifies Figure 5.4 in two ways. First, it adds a second level of partitioning (Order_Number), and reduces the number of Order_Date partitions so that the total number of partitions stays within the limit of 65,535.

```
CREATE TABLE Order_Table ...
PRIMARY INDEX (Customer_Number)
PARTITION BY
        RANGE_N (Order_Date BETWEEN DATE '2010-01-01'
        AND DATE '2011-12-31'          /*24 partitions defined based */
        EACH INTERVAL '1' MONTH),      /*on (1) month intervals */
        RANGE_N( Order_Number
       BETWEEN  122000 and 124000 EACH 1;
                                        /*2000 partitions defined */
```

Figure 5.5

The following example specifies the maximum of 65,535 (3*5*17*257) partitions allowed for two-byte partitioning in a combined partitioning expression.

Because none of the partitioning columns is a component of the primary index, that index cannot be defined as a UPI.

```
CREATE TABLE markets
(productid INTEGER NOT NULL
,region BYTEINT NOT NULL
,activity_date DATE FORMAT 'yyyy-mm-dd' NOT NULL
,revenue_code BYTEINT NOT NULL
,business_sector BYTEINT NOT NULL
,note VARCHAR(256)
)
PRIMARY INDEX (productid, region)
PARTITION BY
        (RANGE_N(region BETWEEN 1 AND 9 EACH 3)
        ,RANGE_N(business_sector BETWEEN 0 AND 49 EACH 10)
        ,RANGE_N(revenue_code BETWEEN 1 AND 34 EACH 2)
        ,RANGE_N(activity_date BETWEEN DATE '1986-01-01'
                                    AND DATE '2007-05-31'
                            EACH INTERVAL '1' MONTH));
```

Figure 5.6

Rules for MLPPI

- Every RANGE_N level must have at least two partitions.
- No more than 15 levels of partitioning are allowed with 2-byte partitioning.
- No more than 62 levels of partitioning are allowed with 8-byte partitioning.
- No more than 65,535 partitions can be defined with 2-byte partitioning.
- No more than 9,223,372,036,854,775,807 partitions can be defined with 8-byte partitioning.

- BLOB, CLOB, and BIGINT are not allowed in partitioning expressions.
- You cannot reference the system-derived PARTITION or PARTITION#L*n* columns in a CREATE JOIN INDEX, CREATE HASH INDEX, or CREATE INDEX requests.
- You can reference the system-derived columns PARTITION#L1 through PARTITION#L15 at any point in a DML request where a table column can be referenced.
- You can also reference the system-derived PARTITION#L*n* columns in the DROP RANGE WHERE clause of an ALTER TABLE request.
- You can neither update these system-derived columns, nor can you assign a value or NULL to them with an insert operation.
- You can qualify the system-derived PARTITION#L*n* columns with a database name and table name just as you can any other table column.
- Also, like the system-derived PARTITION column of single-level PPI tables, the values of the system-derived PARTITION#L*n* columns consume no space in the table. When you reference a PARTITION#L*n* column, the system extracts the internal partition number for the combined partitioning expression from the row and converts it to the external partition number for the corresponding level of the system-derived column.
- A system-derived PARTITION#L*n* column is equivalent to a value expression in which the value expression is identical to the partitioning expression at the specified level defined for the primary index.
- Like the system-derived PARTITION column for single-level PPI tables, the system derived PARTITION#L*n* columns are not included in the list of columns returned by specifying an

ASTERISK character or table_name.* when you select rows from a table.

- You can explicitly select system-derived PARTITION#L*n* column from the table.
- You cannot access the system-derived PARTITION#L*n* columns through a view based on an underlying MLPPI table unless that view explicitly includes the name of the system-derived column in its definition.
- Like the system-derived PARTITION column for single-level PPI tables, the system does not return any system-derived PARTITION#L*n* columns in response to a HELP TABLE or HELP COLUMN request because they are derived and are not stored in the dictionary as names of physical columns in the table.
- Note that if you use ALTER TABLE to change one or more of the partitioning expressions for the primary index of an MLPPI table, the values of the system-derived PARTITION#L*n* columns for rows in the altered table might change.

Partition Ordering

The order of partitioning expressions can be important for multilevel partitioning. The system maps multilevel partitioning expressions into a single-level combined partitioning expression. It then maps the resulting combined partition number 1-to-1 to an internal partition number. Rows are in logical RowID order, where a RowID consists of an internal partition number, a row hash value, and a row uniqueness value. See Figure 4.1.

Partition elimination at the lowest levels can increase overhead because of the frequent need to skip to the next internal partition to be read. This is because a partition at a lower level is split among the partitions at higher levels in the partition hierarchy. At higher levels in the partition hierarchy, there are more contiguous internal partitions to scan and skip.

Columnar Partitioning

Not only can you do row partitioning on tables and join indexes, you can also partition them on their columns. Columnar partitioning is only possible when a MULTISET table or MULTISET join index has no primary Index.

The best workloads for columnar partitioning are those which access a significant number of rows but only project a few columns, or those which access a few rows but project many columns.

COLUMN / ROW

There are two ways the system can format the storage of a columnar partition.

If you specify the COLUMN format, the system creates containers for the specified column(s).

If you specify the ROW format, the system creates subrow(s) for the specified columns. A subrow has the same format as traditional database rows, but only contains the column(s) for the defined partition. Autocompression cannot be defined for subrows.

If you do not specify either, then the system will determine the format based upon the width of the column partition.

In general, the system assigns COLUMN format to narrow partitions and ROW format to wide partitions.

The first example below, defines a column-partitioned table with a USI on column *fips_code*. Each column except for *comment_text* is contained in its own partition, is stored using system-determined COLUMN format, and is autocompressed. Column *comment_text* put in its own partition and is stored using ROW format without autocompression.

```
create table states_part
(state_code char(2)
,fips_code char(2)
,state_name char(25)
,ROW( comment_text varchar(150)) NO AUTO COMPRESS)
PARTITION BY COLUMN,
unique index ( fips_code );
```

Figure 5.7

The difference for the second example is the absence of the ROW specification for *comment_text* in the column list. It is replaced by an ALL BUT (ROW(comment_text)) specification in the PARTITION BY COLUMN clause.

```
create table states_part
(state_code char(2)
,fips_code char(2)
,state_name char(25)
,comment_text varchar(150))
PARTITION BY COLUMN
ALL BUT (ROW(comment_text) NO AUTO COMPRESS),
unique index ( fips_code );
```

Figure 5.8

The next example is another way of defining the same table.

```
create table states_part
(state_code char(2)
,fips_code char(2)
,state_name char(25)
,comment_text varchar(150))
PARTITION BY COLUMN (state_code, fips_code, state_name,
ROW comment_text NO AUTO COMPRESS),
unique index ( fips_code );
```

Figure 5.9

This example defines a column-partitioned table with 3 partitions, one with COLUMN format and two with ROW format.

```
create table example
(a1 bigint
,b1 varchar(300)
,b2 varchar(300)
,b3 varchar(300)
,c1 timestamp(6)
,c2 timestamp(6)
)
PARTITION BY COLUMN
(ROW (a1)              --Explicit ROW, single column
,COLUMN (b1, b2, b3)   --Explicit COLUMN, 3 columns
,ROW (c1, c2)          --Explicit ROW, 2 columns
);
```

Figure 5.10

Making a Choice

If the system-determined format for a column isn't COLUMN, and you determine that it would be a better choice, then specify COLUMN explicitly when you create or alter the table, as show in Figure 5.10. For example, if a column is defined as VARCHAR CHARACTER SET GRAPHIC, or VARBYTE, the system may default to ROW format because of the maximum value length, even though the actual values are small.

The same thing holds true for changing COLUMN to ROW format.

You control which columns go into a partition through the use of parenthesis. As an example, the next figure shows the same table with different partitioning.

```
ct test1(c1 int, c2 int, c3 int,c4 int, c5 int, c6 int) partition by column;
ct test1((c1 int, c2 int, c3 int),(c4 int, c5 int, c6 int)) partition by column.
ct test1((c1 int, c2 int), (c3 int, c4 int), (c5 int, c6 int)) partition by column;
```

Figure 5.11

The first one creates 6 individual partitions, one for each column. The second creates 2 partitions, each containing 3 columns. The third creates 2 partitions containing 3 columns each.

Column partitioned tables and column partitioned join indexes can have one or more row partitioning levels.

For queries that access the same table, but the columns accessed vary from request to request, consider putting the frequently accessed columns into the same partition. If queries don't access the columns frequently, and autocompression of the individual columns or subset is not effective, place those columns into the same partition.

The expected use for column-partitioned tables is to load them using an INSERT / SELECT, run data mining analytics, and then drop the table or selected partitions. This type of table is called an "insert once" table, and is not intended for OLTP applications.

Determining the Rows in Each Partition

There is an internal field named "PARTITION" which will return the system partition number in which a row exists. The following example loads some rows into the Part_X table created in Figure 5.4, and then retrieves all of them along with their PARTITION number:

```
INSERT INTO part_x VALUES(1,1,1,5);
INSERT INTO part_x VALUES(1,1,2,5);
INSERT INTO part_x VALUES(1,2,1,5);
INSERT INTO part_x VALUES(1,2,2,5);
INSERT INTO part_x VALUES(2,1,1,5);
INSERT INTO part_x VALUES(2,1,2,5);
INSERT INTO part_x VALUES(2,2,1,5);
INSERT INTO part_x VALUES(2,2,2,5);

SELECT c1, c2, c3, c4, PARTITION
FROM part_x
ORDER BY PARTITION;

  c1    c2    c3    c4    PARTITION
----  ----  ----  ----  -----------
   1     1     1     5            1
   1     1     2     5            2
   1     2     1     5            3
   1     2     2     5            4
   2     1     1     5            5
   2     1     2     5            6
   2     2     1     5            7
   2     2     2     5            8
```

Figure 5.12

There are additional system-derived columns, PARTITION#L1 through PARTITION#L15 that can be used to locate the rows of a specific partition.

```
SELECT c1, c2, c3, c4, PARTITION
FROM part_x
WHERE part_x.PARTITION#L2 = 1
ORDER BY PARTITION;

  c1    c2    c3    c4    PARTITION
----  ----  ----  ----  -----------
   1     1     1     5            1
   1     1     2     5            2
   2     1     1     5            5
   2     1     2     5            6
```

Figure 5.13

This is the equivalent of the following code:

```
SELECT c1, c2, c3, c4, PARTITION
FROM part_x
WHERE c2 = 1
ORDER BY PARTITION;
```

Figure 5.14

Altering PPI Tables to Add or Delete Partitions

ALTER TABLE [databasename.]tablename DROP RANGE [#Ln] BETWEEN *start_expression* AND *end_expression* EACH *range_size* ;

- Use this form of the ALTER statement to drop a set of ranges from the RANGE_N function on which the partitioning expression for the table is based.
- #L*n* represents a partition level number where *n* is an integer between 1 and 15, inclusive.

- The expressions *start_expression* and *end_expression* are defined using the RANGE_N function.
- Ranges must be specified in ascending order.

ALTER TABLE [databasename.]tablename ADD RANGE [#L*n*] BETWEEN *start_expression* AND *end_expression* EACH *range_size* ;

- Use this form of the ALTER statement to add a set of ranges to the RANGE_N function on which the partitioning expression for the table is based.
- #L*n* represents a partition level number where *n* is an integer between 1 and 15, inclusive.
- The expressions *start_expression* and *end_expression* are defined using the RANGE_N function.
- The expressions must not have a BLOB, CLOB, or BIGINT data type.
- The *range_size* variable must be a constant expression.
- You can also add NO RANGE OR UNKNOWN and UNKNOWN specifications to the definition for the RANGE_N function.
- You can only add ranges if the partitioning expression for the table is derived exclusively from a RANGE_N function.
- Ranges must be specified in ascending order.

ALTER TABLE TO CURRENT

ALTER TABLE *join_index_name* TO CURRENT;

ALTER TABLE *table_name* TO CURRENT;

ALTER TABLE *table_name* TO CURRENT
WITH INSERT INTO *save_table*; /* null partition handler */

ALTER TABLE *table_name* TO CURRENT
        WITH DELETE; /* null partition handler */

This command reconciles the row partitioning for a table or uncompressed join index to a newly resolved date or timestamp when its partitioning is based on the DATE, CURRENT_DATE, or CURRENT_TIMESTAMP functions.

When you build your partitioning expressions, you should specify modified functions such as:

> DATE - INTERVAL '2' DAY, CURRENT_DATE - INTERVAL '2' DAY

However, some other appropriate adjustment rather than specifying an unmodified DATE or CURRENT_DATE function could be as follows:

> RANGE_N (BETWEEN CURRENT_DATE AND DATE '2013-12-31')).

Because requests might be submitted in different time zones than the session time zone in which the ALTER TABLE TO CURRENT request is submitted. Such adjustments ensure that the Optimizer query plans remain the same for the same request regardless of the session time zone.

Specifying a partitioning expression that uses a CURRENT_TIMESTAMP function avoids the time zone issues that occur with partitioning expressions that use a DATE or CURRENT_DATE function, and these partitioning expressions do not require any adjustments to be universally applicable.

Be aware that using an ALTER TABLE TO CURRENT request to reconcile rows with newly resolved DATE, CURRENT_DATE, or CURRENT_TIMESTAMP values in their partitioning expressions can be expensive, both because of the time required to scan a table or join index to find rows that need to be reconciled and because of the time required to move or delete rows that need to be reconciled if you specify a WITH DELETE or WITH INSERT null partition handler clause with the ALTER TABLE TO CURRENT request for a table. You cannot specify a null partition handler for an ALTER TABLE TO CURRENT request made on a join index, since the system cannot remove rows from a join index.

If a newly resolved date evaluates the starting expression (containing the DATE or CURRENT_DATE function) of a RANGE_N function to a partition boundary, Teradata Database drops all of the partitions that are earlier than this partition. Otherwise, Teradata Database repartitions the entire table using the new partitioning expression.

For example, consider the following CREATE TABLE request submitted on April 1, 2006.

```
CREATE TABLE ppi (
i INTEGER,
j DATE)
PRIMARY INDEX(i)
PARTITION BY RANGE_N(j BETWEEN CURRENT_DATE
AND CURRENT_DATE+INTERVAL'1' YEAR -
INTERVAL'1' DAY
EACH INTERVAL'1' MONTH);
```

Figure 5.15

In this example, consider the last resolved date to be April 1, 2006 and assume that, when the value for DATE or CURRENT_DATE is DATE '2006-06-01', you submit an ALTER TABLE TO CURRENT request. The starting expression with the newly resolved DATE or CURRENT_DATE value falls on a partition boundary of the third partition; therefore, Teradata Database drops partitions 1 and 2, and the last reconciled date is set to the newly resolved value for DATE or CURRENT_DATE.

Now suppose you submit an ALTER TABLE TO CURRENT request on DATE '2006-06-10'. The starting expression with the newly resolved DATE or CURRENT_DATE value does *not* fall on a partition boundary, so Teradata Database scans all of the rows, and repartitions them based on the new partitioning expression. The partition boundary after this request aligns to the tenth day of a month instead of the earlier first day of a month.

With an updatable DATE or CURRENT_DATE value in a partitioning expression, it becomes possible for a partitioning expression based on a RANGE_N function to become obsolete after some time passes. Exercise great caution specifying RANGE_N functions for such cases, only doing so after you fully understand its implications for reconciliation and its applicability as the value changes each time you reconcile the DATE, CURRENT_DATE, or CURRENT_TIMESTAMP value. For example, consider the following CREATE TABLE request.

```
CREATE TABLE ppi (
i INTEGER,
j DATE)
PRIMARY INDEX(i)
PARTITION BY RANGE_N(j BETWEEN CURRENT_DATE
AND DATE '2008-01-01'
EACH INTERVAL '1' MONTH);
```

Figure 5.16

If you reconcile this table using an ALTER TABLE TO CURRENT request after January 1, 2008, the request aborts and Teradata Database returns an error to the requestor because all the defined ranges are null.

Although you can specify the DATE, CURRENT_DATE, or CURRENT_TIMESTAMP functions anywhere in a partitioning expression that a date or timestamp constant is valid, you must take appropriate caution in doing so.

ALTER TABLE vs. CREATE TABLE

There are three ways to redefine the PRIMARY INDEX/NO PRIMARY INDEX and PARTITION BY/NOT PARTITIONED clauses for a table.

- Use the MODIFY PRIMARY INDEX syntax for ALTER TABLE to modify the primary index for the table.
  - If you only need to change the partitioning for a table, you can optionally specify MODIFY without also specifying PRIMARY INDEX. The PRIMARY INDEX keywords are only required to modify the primary index of a table.
- Create a new table with the primary index or partitioning defined properly and then use an INSERT... SELECT to copy the data from the old table to the new table.
- Use the CREATE TABLE AS to do the following operations.
  - Create a new table with the primary index and partitioning, if required, defined properly. If the new table is to be column-partitioned, create a new column-partitioned table with no primary index.
  - Copy the rows and, if desired, the statistics from the old table into the new table.

Using ALTER TABLE

You can use ALTER TABLE to perform the following modifications to primary indexes and partitioning for a table that is populated or empty.

- To change a NUPI to a UPI, specify MODIFY UNIQUE PRIMARY INDEX.
- To change a UPI to a NUPI, specify MODIFY NOT UNIQUE PRIMARY INDEX.
- Add or drop partitioning expression ranges, specify ADD RANGE or DROP RANGE.

- Validate partitioning by regenerating table headers and correcting any errors in row partitioning, specify REVALIDATE PRIMARY INDEX.

The following ALTER TABLE modifications can only be done to an empty table.

- To change a partitioned object to an unpartitioned object, specify NOT PARTITIONED.
- To change an unpartitioned object to a partitioned object, specify PARTITION BY.
- Add or drop primary index columns, specify MODIFY or MODIFY PRIMARY INDEX.

Performance Implications of Altering a Primary Index Using ALTER TABLE Requests

You should consider the following information about the immediate performance impact of altering the primary index for a table to best schedule the operation in a way that has the least impact on your production workload.

- Altering an empty table is fairly quick.
- Altering a primary-indexed table to have a unique or non-unique primary index is fairly quick.
- Altering a primary-indexed table to change the primary index name is fairly quick.
- The following cumulative performance issues are all concerned with dropping or adding new ranges or partitions to a row-partitioned table.
    - When dropping or adding new ranges or partitions for a populated table, the operation can be fairly quick because rows that remain in the retained ranges and partitions need not be processed or repartitioned.

- There is an additional small overhead if dropped ranges and partitions are populated, and still further overhead if any referential integrity constraints are defined on the table.
- There is additional overhead if new ranges are added and there are populated NO RANGE [OR UNKNOWN) or UNKNOWN partitions or rows in dropped ranges that need to be moved to the added ranges because rows must be processed to determine if any of them need to be assigned to one of the new ranges and, if so, to move them to the correct range.
- You must update any secondary, join, or hash indexes on the table.

  Updating secondary, join, and hash indexes can be lengthy operations and depend on several factors, including the size of the table and indexes and the number of rows deleted or moved.
- There is additional overhead if the deleted rows are inserted into a save table. The degree of this overhead depends on the number of rows that must be inserted into the save table and the other standard performance issues associated with inserting rows into a table.
- If a table is defined with a NO RANGE partition, specifying a WITH DELETE or WITH INSERT INTO clause in an ALTER TABLE request used to change its definition has no effect.

  In this case, rows from deleted partitions and rows whose partition number evaluates to something other than 1 - 65,535, inclusive, for 2-byte partitioning or something other than 1 - 9,223,372,036,854,775,805, inclusive, for 8-byte partitioning, are retained in the NO RANGE partition rather than being moved to the target table specified in the WITH DELETE or WITH INSERT INTO clause.

Using CREATE TABLE

To redefine the primary index or partitioning for a table without using an ALTER TABLE request, perform one of the following procedures.

- First method.
    - Copy the table into a newly created table defined with a different primary index (or with no primary index) and populate it using the CREATE TABLE ... AS syntax.
    - Catalog the privileges on the old table.
    - Drop the original table.
    - Rename the new table.
    - Grant privileges on the new table.
- Second method.
    - Using a different name, create a new table that specifies the new index.
    - Populate the new table using an INSERT ... SELECT request.
    - Catalog the privileges on the old table.
    - Drop the original table.
    - Rename the new table
    - Grant privileges on the new table.

NO CASE, NO RANGE, or UNKNOWN

The following refers to the example that appeared as Figure 5.1, which defines just three partitions. The problem is that any row with a NULL Order_Total, or Order_Total equal to or greater than 100000 will be rejected because there isn't a partition for them:

```
CREATE TABLE Order_Table ...
PRIMARY INDEX (customer_number)
PARTITION BY CASE_N (Order_Total < 1000,      /* 1st partition */
                     Order_Total < 10000,     /* 2nd partition */
                     Order_Total < 100000);   /* 3rd partition */
```

Figure 5.17

The system provides two additional tests named NO CASE and UNKNOWN. The NO CASE partition will receive any row with an Order_Total equal to or greater than 100000, and UNKNOWN will receive any rows having a NULL Order_Total since you can't say that NULL is less than 1000.

```
CREATE TABLE Order_Table ...
PRIMARY INDEX (customer_number)
PARTITION BY CASE_N (Order_Total < 1000,      /* 1st partition */
                     Order_Total < 10000,     /* 2nd partition */
                     Order_Total < 100000,    /* 3rd partition */
                     NO CASE,                 /* => 100000  */
                     UNKNOWN);                /* NULL */
```

Figure 5.18

In the next example, NO CASE and UNKNOWN have been combined into a single partition:

```
CREATE TABLE Order_Table ...
PRIMARY INDEX (customer_number)
PARTITION BY CASE_N (Order_Total < 1000,     /* 1st partition */
                     Order_Total < 10000,    /* 2nd partition */
                     Order_Total < 100000,   /* 3rd partition */
            NO CASE OR UNKNOWN);        /* => 100,000 & NULL */
```

Figure 5.19

There are comparable tests for RANGE_N partitions, NO RANGE and UNKNOWN. The following example takes the table from Figure 5.4 and modifies it to capture (rather than reject) rows having partition values less than 1 or greater than 2. By declaring a partitioning column NOT NULL, the UNKNOWN test can be eliminated.

```
CREATE TABLE part_x
(c1 BYTEINT NOT NULL
,c2 BYTEINT NOT NULL
,c3 BYTEINT
,c4 BYTEINT NOT NULL)
PRIMARY INDEX (c1, c2, c3)
PARTITION BY (RANGE_N(c1 BETWEEN 1 AND 2 EACH 1, NO RANGE)
             ,RANGE_N(c2 BETWEEN 1 AND 2 EACH 1, NO RANGE)
             ,RANGE_N(c3 BETWEEN 1 AND 2 EACH 1
                      NO RANGE, UNKNOWN));
```

Figure 5.20

Join Considerations and PPI

Joins can be different for PPI and NPPI tables that are otherwise equivalent, but in many cases the effect of the different join strategies that arise cannot easily be predicted.

The join plan that the Optimizer pursues depends on the picture it has of the data demographics based on collected statistics, random-AMP samples, and derived statistics. The usual recommendation applies here -- check EXPLAIN reports to determine the best way to design your indexes to achieve the optimal join geography.

The following design considerations are important for this PPI performance characteristic:

- PI-to-PI joins are more likely to generate different join plans than PPI-to-NPPI join comparisons.
- To minimize the potential for performance issues in making PI-to-PI joins, consider the following guidelines:
    - Partition the two tables identically if possible.
    - A coarser granularity of the PPI partitions is likely to be superior to a finer partition granularity.
    - Examine your EXPLAIN reports to determine which join methods the Optimizer is selecting to join the tables.
    - RowKey PPI table joins are generally better than joins based on another family of join methods.
    - Efficient partition elimination can often convert joins that would otherwise be poor performers into good performers.
    - The most likely candidate for poor join performance is found when you are joining a PPI table with an NPPI table, the PPI table partitioning column set is not defined in the NPPI table, there are no predicates on the PPI table partitioning column set and there are many partitions defined for the PPI table.
    - Specify equijoins on the primary index and partitioning column sets, if possible, in order to prejudice the Optimizer to use efficient RowKey-based joins.
    - Consider including the partitioning column in the NPPI table so you can join on the partition column. This means that, depending on the situation, you might want

to consider denormalizing the physical schema to enhance the performance of PPI-NPPI table joins.

- If you specify an equijoin on the primary index column set, but not on the partitioning column set, the fewer combined partitions that exist after any partition elimination, the better. Otherwise, the table might need to be spooled and sorted.
- The Optimizer can specify Sliding Window Joins when there are a small number of combined partitions.
- Use RANGE_N to define fewer partitions and specify conditions on the partitioning columns to reduce the number of combined partitions involved in the join by evoking partition elimination.
- The Optimizer does not know whether a combined partition is empty or not, so it has to assume that all defined combined partitions might have rows with respect to the plan it generates; however, it might choose among several such plans based on the estimated number of populated combined partitions.
- Dynamic Partition Elimination for a Product Join improves performance when a PPI table and another table are equijoined on the partitioning column of the PPI table.
- Remember to collect statistics on all of the following:
  - The primary indexes of both tables.
  - The partitioning column of the PPI table.
  - The column in the NPPI table that is equated to the partitioning column of the PPI table.
  - The system-derived PARTITION column of the PPI table.

PPI Advantages

- Partition elimination enables large performance gains to be realizable, and these are visible to end users. For this particular optimization, more populated partitions are generally better than fewer populated partitions.

- Batch inserts and updates can run faster if the partitioning schema matches the data arrival pattern. This optimization is visible only to the DBA and operations staff.
- Finer granularity of partitions is generally better than a coarser granularity: daily is better than monthly.
- The largest performance improvements occur when there are no secondary indexes.
- TPump inserts and updates can benefit from more FSG cache hits. Typically, a finer partition granularity is better than a coarser one.
- Inserts into empty partitions are not journaled. This optimization is only invoked if the table has no referential integrity constraints.
- Delete operations can be nearly instantaneous when the partitioning column set matches the retention policy, there is no secondary index defined on the PPI column set, and the delete is the last statement in the transaction.
- You can delete all of the rows in a partition if you want to do so. In this case, there is no journaling of rows if no secondary index is defined on the PPI column set.

PPI Limitations

- PPI table rows are each 2 bytes or 8 bytes wider than the equivalent NPPI table row. The extra bytes are used to store the partition number for the row.
- You cannot define the primary index of a PPI to be unique unless the entire partitioning column set is part of the primary index definition. You *can* define a USI on the primary index columns to enforce uniqueness if the complete partitioning column set is not a component of the primary index definition;

however, that adds different performance issues to the equation.

- Primary index-based row access can be degraded if the partitioning column set is not a component of the primary index.
- If you can define a secondary index on the primary index column set, then performance is independent of the number of partitions.
- If you cannot, or have not, defined a secondary index on the primary index, then having fewer partitions is better than having more partitions, whether achieved by means of the table definition itself or by partition elimination during query processing.
- Joins of PPI tables to NPPI tables with the same primary index can be degraded. To combat this, observe the following guidelines:
    - Identically partition all tables to be joined with the same primary index when possible and then join them on the partitioning columns.
    - Fewer partitions, whether achieved by means of the table definition itself or by partition elimination, are often better than more partitions for the NPPI-to-PPI join scenario.
- You *cannot* use sampling to collect COLUMN statistics for the partitioning columns of PPI tables and you *should not* use sampling to collect INDEX statistics for those columns. Instead, collect statistics on the system-derived PARTITION or PARTITION#L*n* columns.

Chapter 5: Practice Questions

1. Given the following partitioning expression, into which partition will state code OR (Oregon) be placed?

   PARTITION BY (CASE_N(state_code IN('HI', 'PR', 'VI'), NO CASE, UNKNOWN))

   a. Partition 1
   b. Partition 2
   c. Partition 3
   d. Partition 4
   e. Partition 5

2. In order to use column partitioning, the table must be a ________.
   a. UPI MULTISET table
   b. NUPI MULTISET table
   c. NoPI MULTISET table
   d. UPI SET table
   e. NUPI SET table

3. Which of the following ALTER TABLE modifications can only be done to an empty table?
   a. To change a partitioned object to an unpartitioned object, specify NOT PARTITIONED
   b. To change a UPI to a NUPI, specify MODIFY NOT UNIQUE PRIMARY INDEX.
   c. Add or drop partitioning expression ranges, specify ADD RANGE or DROP RANGE.
   d. Validate partitioning by regenerating table headers and correcting any errors in row partitioning, specify REVALIDATE PRIMARY INDEX.

4. What is the valid range of partitioning levels for 2-byte partitioning?
   a. 7
   b. 15
   c. 31
   d. 63

Chapter Notes

Utilize this space for notes, key points to remember, diagrams, areas of further study, etc.

Chapter 6: Secondary Indexes

Certification Objectives

- ✓ Given a scenario, identify when to create an index that cover queries.
- ✓ Given a scenario, identify when to use NUSIs.
- ✓ Given a scenario, identify when to use USIs.
- ✓ Explain the effects of the Primary Key and Unique constraints on physical design.

Before You Begin

You should be familiar with the following terms and concepts.

Terms	Key Concepts
Secondary Indexes	Understand the types and options
USI	Considerations for utilizing a USI
NUSI	When to implement and best practices
Bit Mapping	How does this work

Secondary Index Subtable

Whenever users access a table using columns that are not the PI, the system has no choice but to do a full table scan. Though the MPP architecture of Teradata makes this operation rapid, for very large tables, response times could run into minutes instead of seconds or sub-seconds.

For this reason, designers will add Secondary Indexes (USI and NUSI) to tables, to speed up access times. The tradeoff is space versus speed. If you wish to save space, then you must tolerate slower response, maintenance, and recovery times. If you want faster access, then you must be willing to have a table require more disk space (extra indexes, Fallback, etc.).

To support Secondary Indexes, the system creates index rows consisting of the index value (one index row per distinct value) and pointers to the corresponding base table rows, and stores them in subtables. When queries supply access values for indexed columns, the system may access the index subtable and use the pointer(s) in the qualifying index row to access the desired base table rows. If the index is a covering index (See Chapter 3 and Covering Indexes later in this chapter), the system may be able to satisfy the query without having to access the base table.

The following figure shows an overview of accessing a table either by its PI or by a Secondary Index.

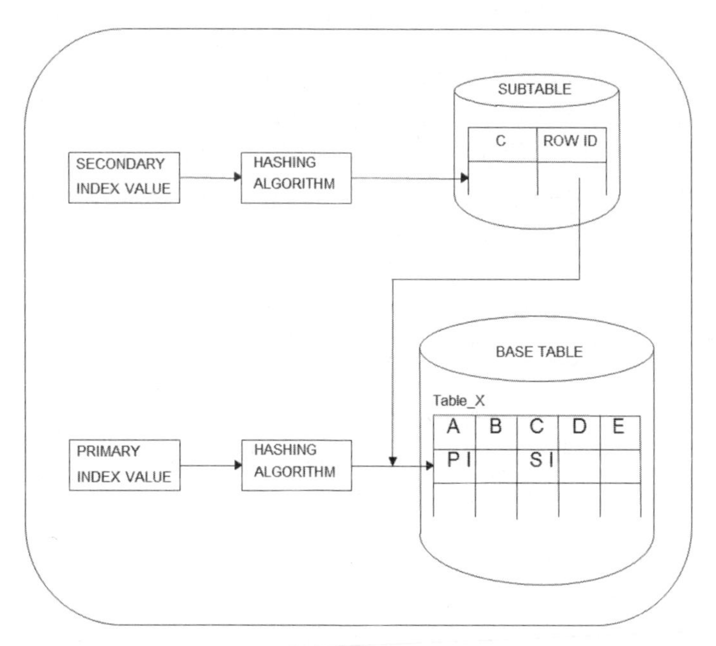

Figure 6.1

Unique Secondary Index (USI)

Like a unique primary index, a unique secondary index can be used to guarantee the uniqueness of each value in a column set. If a table has a NUPI, a USI can be used to enforce the uniqueness of the PK. When a non-primary index uniqueness constraint is created for a table, the system implements it as a USI.

The index rows for a USI are globally distributed across the AMPs based on the index value's row hash. There will be one index row for each base table row.

Unique Secondary Index Walkthrough

When a query accesses a USI column set with an equality value, the system hashes the value and uses that row hash to find the corresponding index row. The process is identical to locating a UPI table row. The index row not only contains a copy of the index value, but the RowID of the corresponding base table row. Since the base table rows and the index rows are hashed on different column sets, they are probably on different AMPs. Even if the index row and base table row are on the same AMP, the system still has to use the BYNET Hash Maps to identify the base table row AMP. USI accesses are always a two-AMP operation. The following shows this process:

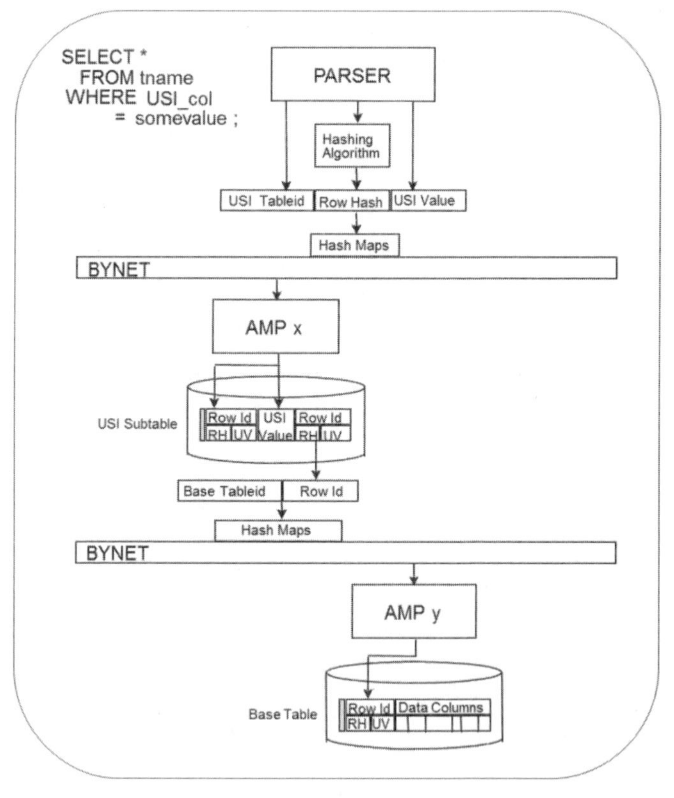

Figure 6.2

Non-Unique Secondary Index (NUSI)

The index rows for a NUSI are NOT distributed globally, but are AMP-local instead. Each AMP scans its set of base table rows and creates an index row for each distinct NUSI value and one or more RowID pointers to the corresponding base table rows on that AMP.

Note: NUSI operations are always an all-AMP operation, both for creation and for access.

Non-Unique Secondary Index Walkthrough

When a query provides an equality access to the NUSI column set, the system hashes the value, and broadcasts it along with the subtable ID and index value to all of the AMPs. Using the Row Hash and index values, each AMP searches its index rows for a match. If an AMP finds an index row, it then uses the RowID pointer list to retrieve its corresponding base table rows. If an AMP fails to find an index row, it sends back a **Not Found** message and is no longer involved in the search. Every AMP must respond to a NUSI query with either a Not Found or its set of selected rows.

The following diagram shows this action. AMPs 1, 2, and 4 find an index row and return their base table rows. AMP 3 fails to find an index row and therefore has no rows to return.

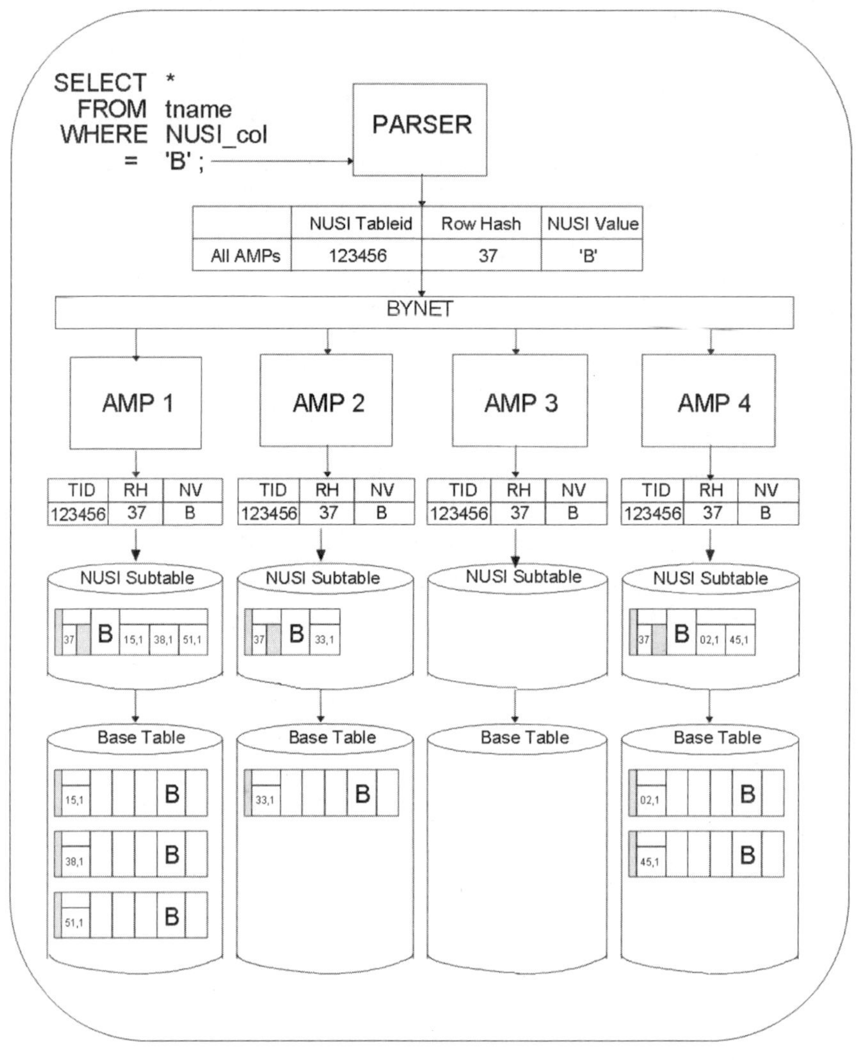

Figure 6.3

Value Ordered Secondary Index

The normal way for the system to store rows is by Row Hash and Uniqueness Value (RowID). This applies to table rows and Secondary Index rows, as shown in the example above (Figure 6.3).

A Value-Ordered NUSI sorts the index rows on the value of the ordering column, not the Row Hash. Ordering is limited to a single numeric or date column that is not more than 4 bytes in size.

Value-ordered NUSIs are very efficient for range conditions. Because the NUSI rows are sorted by data value, it is possible to search only a portion of the index subtable for a given range of key values.

Value Ordered NUSI Walkthrough

The following diagram (Figure 6.4) shows an example of one AMP's set of table rows, and then it shows the normal hash-ordered NUSI subtable rows followed by value-ordered NUSI rows. Remember, NUSI rows are AMP-local.

Notice that the same data value (e.g. PI=100 and NUSI =100) stored in the same data type (INT) always produces the same Row Hash value (14357).

CREATE TABLE t1 (c1 INT, c2 INT, c3 INT) UNIQUE PRIMARY INDEX (c1);

Single AMP's Base Table Rows

14357	1	100	300	200
14357	2	655	250	616
77450	1	300	100	655
23487	1	565	250	787
46289	1	193	300	200
33666	1	268	323	655

CREATE INDEX (c2) ON t1;

NUSI Subtable Rows

13336	1	250	14357	2	23487	1
14357	1	100	77450	1		
77450	1	323	33666	1		
77450	2	300	14357	1	46289	1

CREATE INDEX (c3) ORDER BY c3 ON t1;

NUSI Subtable Rows

62244	1	200	14357	1	46289	1
88212	1	616	14357	2		
14357	2	655	33666	1	77450	1
11128	1	787	23487	1		

Figure 6.4

Non-Unique Secondary Indexes and Statistics

The Parser needs accurate statistics to decide whether or not to use a NUSI. Just because a NUSI exists, doesn't mean it will be used if a full table scan would be less costly.

If a NUSI is created and dropped frequently, consider collecting statistics on the base table columns. The Parser will always substitute base table statistics if statistics haven't been collected on an index.

If you use the CREATE INDEX form of the COLLECT STATISTICS statement, statistics can be collected for all indexes in one SQL statement.

Note: See Chapter 16 for more on Statistics.

NUSI Bit Mapping

When statistics have been collected on NUSI indexed columns, the Optimizer might consider using a NUSI Bit Mapping operation in its query plan. NUSI Bit Mapping is a mechanism that intersects the data values to determine if common Row IDs exists between multiple NUSI values. When the query utilizes several weakly selective indexes that are strongly selective together, the Optimizer will most likely choose a NUSI Bit Mapping operation, which reduces the number of base rows that are accessed in the result set.

This approach can achieve significant performance improvement because it reduces the number of base table I/Os and is much faster than copying, sorting, and comparing the Row ID lists.

At least two NUSI equality conditions are required in order for NUSI Bit Mapping to be considered. In addition, all NUSIs in the query must be linked together using the AND operator. Finally, all of the conditions in the WHERE/AND clause must yield an amount of rows that is less than one row per data block.

Strongly selective NUSI = Rows/Value < Data Blocks/AMP

A weakly selective NUSI accesses one or more rows per data block. If all of the data blocks would have to be accessed, the Optimizer will ignore the NUSI (and its processing overhead) and perform a full-table scan.

Weakly selective NUSI = Rows/Value >= 1 Data Block/AMP

Note: Any OR operators in the query will almost always result in the Optimizer choosing a full table scan. An EXPLAIN on the query can determine if a query utilizes NUSI Bit Mapping. See the join chapter for more information on how to determine NUSI Bit Mapping with the EXPLAIN statement.

Covering Indexes

The Optimizer aggressively pursues NUSIs when they cover a query. The expression *covering* means that all of the columns requested in a query are also available from an existing index subtable, making it unnecessary to access the base table rows to complete the query. Some vendors refer to this as index-only access.

Covering of a query can also be partial, or an index can fail to cover any aspect of a query.

In the case of a partial covering index for single-table access, the system can get the row IDs for those base table rows that possibly qualify for a query by preliminary examination from the index, but then must also access the base table itself to retrieve the definitively qualified rows.

Even a partial index cover can accelerate the processing of a query, especially when the base table being accessed is very large and the query constraints on the partially covering NUSI are highly selective.

The Optimizer also selects a secondary index to process an aggregation on indexed values if the index covers the necessary values.

If an aggregate join index covers the query, the Optimizer selects it for the access plan before considering a secondary index.

A NUSI covers a query if any of the following criteria are true:

- The query does not reference any columns other than those in the NUSI.
- The NUSI includes all columns in the base table referenced in a query and any of the following criteria are true:
    - The query does not reference a character column set that is not defined as either CASESPECIFIC or UPPERCASE in the base table.
      Teradata Database converts such character column data to UPPERCASE when it stores it in the subtable of a NUSI defined without the ALL option. The stored data might be different from the original lowercase data stored in the base table.
    - This NUSI is defined with the ALL option.
    - This NUSI is *not* defined with the ALL option, but does not contain any bad character column sets. (A bad character is one that causes an error with a valid FORMAT or a character-to-numeric conversion.)
    - This NUSI is *not* defined with the ALL option, *and* it contains a bad character column set, *but* the bad character columns are only specified in a COUNT function or UPPERCASE operator in the query.

    - This NUSI is *not* defined with the ALL option *and* it contains a bad character column set, *and* the bad character column set is not specified other than in a COUNT function or UPPERCASE operator in the select list, *and* there is no CASESPECIFIC condition on the bad character column set in the conditions of the query.

A partially-covering NUSI is one that does not fully cover a query, but *does* satisfy both of the following criteria:

- Some single-table constraints of the query contain the NUSI column set.
- The NUSI contains a bad character column set, *and* the query does not specify an inequality CASESPECIFIC condition on the bad character column set, *and* no CASE expression is specified in a query condition that also specifies the bad character column set.

The Optimizer attempts to use index covering for its query plans even when classical indexing techniques do not apply because scanning an index is almost always faster than scanning the base table it references and the enhanced efficiency can result in significantly faster retrieval.

Chapter 6: Practice Questions

1. A "bad character" in a covering NUSI is ___________ or ___________. (Choose 2)
   a. one that causes an error on a character-to-numeric conversion
   b. one that has an outstanding felony arrest warrant
   c. one that causes an error on a numeric-to-character conversion
   d. one that causes an error on a UNICODE to LATIN conversion
   e. one that causes an error with a valid FORMAT clause

2. Given the following table and query, which phrase best describes the NUSI?

```
create table t1(c1 int, c2 int, c3 int, c4 int, c5 int)
primary index(c1) index(c3, c4, c5);

select c5, c3, c4 from t1;
```

   a. Covering USI
   b. Non-covering NUSI
   c. Covering NUSI
   d. Partial covering NUSI

3. Which expression describes a strongly selective NUSI?
   a. Data Blocks/AMP < Rows/Value
   b. Data Blocks/AMP > Rows/Value
   c. Rows/Value = Data Blocks/AMP
   d. Rows/Value > Data Blocks/AMP

4. Indicate the number of AMPs involved in each of the following operations.

	SQL Statement	
a.	create table t1(c1 int, c2 int, c3 int) primary index (c1);	
b.	create unique index (c2) on t1;	
c.	create index (c3) on t1;	
d.	select * from t1 where c2 = 123;	
e.	select * from t1 where c3 = 456;	
f.	select * from t1 where c1 = 321;	

Chapter Notes

Utilize this space for notes, key points to remember, diagrams, areas of further study, etc.

Chapter 7: Denormalization Techniques

Certification Objectives

- ✓ Describe the temporary table options and their advantages and disadvantages.
- ✓ Describe the effect of denormalization on data integration.
- ✓ Identify the types of derived data and how to manage them.
- ✓ Determine when denormalization may be appropriate.

Before You Begin

You should be familiar with the following terms and concepts.

Terms	Key Concepts
Derived Data	Types of derived data
Pre-joining Tables	Considerations for utilization and performance impacts
Summary Tables	Reasons for implementation
Temporary Tables	How to configure and best practices

Derived Data

Derived attributes are attributes that are not atomic. Their data can be derived from atomic attributes in the database. Because they are not atomic, they violate the rules of normalization.

Derived attributes fall into two basic types:

- Summary (aggregate) data
- Data that can be directly derived from other attributes

Storing derived data violates first normal form. There are occasions when you might want to denormalize standalone calculations for performance reasons. The decision to denormalize should be based on the following demographic information, all of which is derived through the ATM process:

- Number of tables and rows involved
- Access frequency
- Data volatility
- Data change schedule

As a general rule, using an aggregate join index or a global temporary table is preferable to denormalizing the physical implementation of the fully normalized logical model.

Storing Aggregates

There are three recommended ways of handling aggregates without denormalizing the logical/physical model.

- Aggregate join indexes
- Global temporary tables with derived column definitions
- Views with derived column definitions

Pre-Joining Tables

Join processing can be very slow and costly, especially on other systems. Denormalizing the model by doing pre-joins has been used as a method to reduce the time and cost of repeatedly joining tables. Though there are valid reasons for denormalizing the model with pre-joins, there are even more reasons not to.

Teradata supports a Join Index. Although join indexes create and manage pre-joins, and optionally aggregates, they do not denormalize the physical implementation of your normalized logical model because they are not a component of the fully normalized logical model.

The following is an example of creating a Join Index:

```
CREATE JOIN INDEX EmployeeJob
AS SELECT (JobCode, JobDescription),
          (EmployeeNumber, EmployeeName)
FROM Job JOIN Employee ON JobCode;
```

Figure 7.1

The above example is a compressed join index. The two fields (in parentheses) are field 1 and field 2 with field 2 being the repeating values for each set of field one.

This join index not only eliminates the possibility for update anomalies, it also reduces storage by compressing redundant Job table information.

Covered Query

Any index (Join, Hash, NUSI) that contains all, or most, of the columns referenced in a query is referred to as a covering index. The system can access the index to satisfy the query, and can also use the index to access the underlying base table(s) for non-indexed column values.

Summary Tables

Another denormalization technique is to create summary tables to hold the results of various calculations. Since summary tables exist outside of the normalized data tables, they can always be rebuilt from the base tables if necessary.

Summary tables can be permanent, derived, volatile temporary or global temporary tables.

Derived Tables

A derived table is one that exists only within a query. It is defined, loaded, used, and dropped all within the same SQL statement. A derived table is obtained from one or more other tables as the result of a subquery.

It eliminates CREATE and DROP TABLE statements for storing retrieved information.

Volatile Temporary Tables

Volatile temporary tables are created by a user using the CREATE VOLATILE TABLE syntax. Once created, it will persist until the user's session ends. At that time, the system will drop its definition and its data.

The definition of a volatile temporary table is not stored in the data dictionary, and space of its data comes from the user's Spool, not from Perm space.

Volatile temporary tables provide a convenient way of passing derived data from one job step to another.

Global Temporary Tables

A global temporary table is defined by the CREATE GLOBAL TEMPORARY TABLE syntax, and its definition is stored in the data dictionary, thereby making the table's definition available to multiple users. A global temporary table is empty until authorized users load data into it, which creates a materialized copy of the table. However, space for that data comes from each user's Temp space, thereby making each user's data private and inaccessible by other users. When a user's session ends, the user's Temp space is released back to the system, effectively deleting the user's materialized copy of the table.

A typical use of a global temporary table is to create a generic report layout table that is used by multiple individuals and groups. The DBA creates the table's definition, and then authorizes its use to the user community.

Denormalization Effects

Denormalize the implementation of the logical model only after you have thoroughly analyzed the costs and benefits, and only after you have completed a normalized logical design.

Consider the following list of effects of denormalization before you decide to undertake design changes:

- A denormalized physical implementation can increase hardware costs. The rows of a denormalized table are always wider than the rows of a fully normalized table. A row cannot span data blocks; therefore, there is a high probability that the system will be forced to use a larger data block size for a denormalized table. The greater the degree of denormalization of a table, the larger the impact on storage space. This impact can be severe in many cases. Row width also affects the transfer rate for all I/O operations; not just for disk access, but also for transmission across the BYNET and to the requesting client.

- While denormalization benefits the applications it is specifically designed to enhance, it often decreases the performance of other applications, thus contravening the goal of maintaining application neutrality for the database.

- A corollary to this observation is the fact that a denormalized database makes it more difficult to implement new, performant applications unless the new applications rely on the same denormalized schema components as existing applications.

- Because of the previous two effects, denormalization often increases the cost and complexity of programming.

- Denormalization introduces update anomalies to the database. Remember that the original impetus behind normalization theory was to eliminate update anomalies.

Teradata continues to introduce functions and facilities that permit you to achieve the performance benefits of denormalization while running under a direct physical implementation of your fully normalized logical model.

Consider one of the following instead of denormalizing your physical data model:

- Views
- Derived tables
- Volatile temporary tables
- Hash and join indexes
- Aggregate join indexes
- Global temporary tables

Chapter 7: Practice Questions

1. Which of the following statements about denormalization is false?
    a. The rows of denormalized tables are generally wider.
    b. Denormalization reduces update anomalies.
    c. Denormalization is application oriented.
    d. Denormalization increases the cost and complexity of programming.

2. Which of the following denormalization techniques exists within the normalized 3NF logical/physical model?
    a. Hash Indexes
    b. Join Indexes
    c. Aggregate Join Indexes
    d. Global Temporary Tables
    e. Repeating Groups

3. Indicate whether Perm, Spool, or Temp space is used for each of the following.
    a. Derived table ___________
    b. MULTISET table _________
    c. SET table _____________
    d. Temporary table ________
    e. Volatile table ___________

Chapter Notes

Utilize this space for notes, key points to remember, diagrams, areas of further study, etc.

Chapter 8: Join Types and Strategies

Certification Objectives

- ✓ Given a scenario, identify a design strategy to efficiently join tables together.
- ✓ Given a scenario, identify if skewed processing will occur.

Before You Begin

You should be familiar with the following terms and concepts.

Terms	Key Concepts
Join Types	Explain the different Join Types
Join Strategies	Understand the differences
Nested Join	Considerations and benefits for using
Product Join	How could this impact performance

Basic Join Example

The typical join is an equijoin between rows having matching data values in the join columns. The rows may be in the same table (self-join) or different tables.

The following is an example of a typical equijoin:

```
SELECT t1.c2, t2.c2, t2.c3
FROM t1 INNER JOIN t2
ON t1.c3 = t2.c3;

-or-

SELECT t1.c2, t2.c2, t2.c3
FROM t1, t2
WHERE t1.c3 = t2.c3;
```

Figure 8.1

Join Types and Strategies

Depending on the indexes defined for the tables involved and whether statistics are available for the indexes, the Optimizer processes a join using one of the following join algorithms:

- Merge Join
- Product Join
- Hash Join
- Nested Join (local and remote)
- Exclusion Join (merge and product)
- Inclusion Join (merge and product)
- RowID Join

Join Strategies: Merge

The Merge Join retrieves rows from two tables or spools and then puts them onto a common AMP based on the row hash of the columns involved in the join. The system sorts the rows into join column row hash sequence, then joins those rows that have matching join column row hash values.

In preparation for this join, the columns on which tables or spools are matched could also be the columns that are redistributed, duplicated, or sorted. Merge Join is generally more efficient than a Product Join because it requires fewer comparisons and because blocks from both tables are read only once.

Join Strategies: Merge Strategy #1

Before two rows can be joined, they must be on the same AMP.

If the join columns are the Primary Indexes of the two tables, matching rows are already on common AMPs. No redistribution is required. The system can proceed directly to the join. Figure 8.2 shows this:

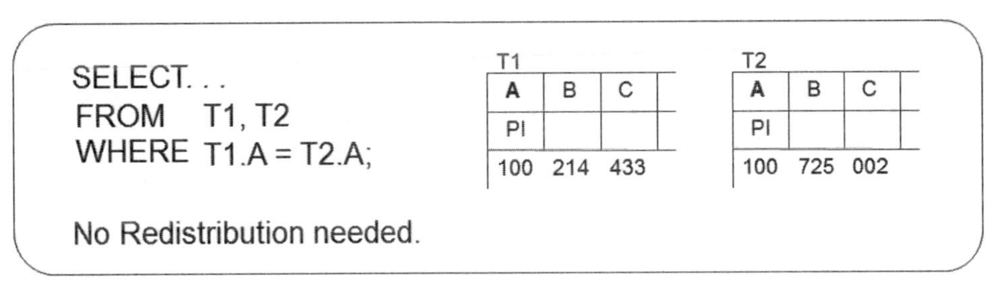

Figure 8.2

Join Strategies: Merge Strategy #2

Before two rows can be joined, they must be on the same AMP.

In the following diagram, the Primary Index of T3 is being joined to a non-Primary Index column. In this case, the system can hash redistribute copies of the T4 rows. Once that step is finished, the system can proceed to the join.

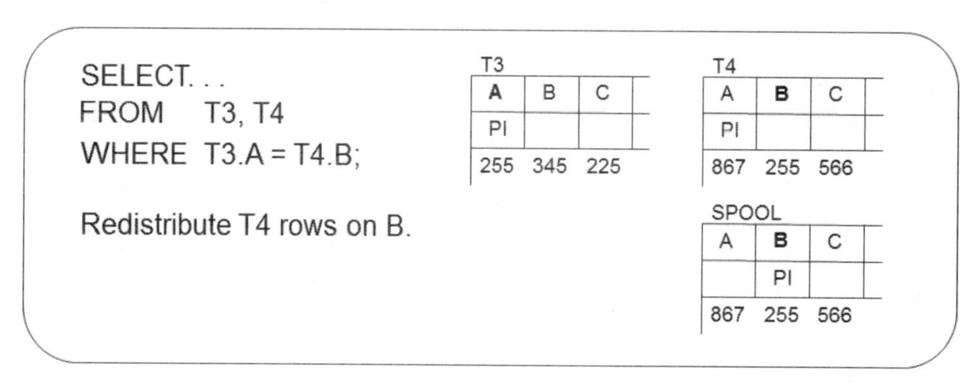

Figure 8.3

Join Strategies: Merge Strategy #3

Before two rows can be joined, they must be on the same AMP.

In this next example, the join columns are not the Primary Index of either table. What the system can do in this case is to hash redistribute copies of both tables based on the row hash of the join column values.

Once the two tables have been redistributed, the system can proceed to the join:

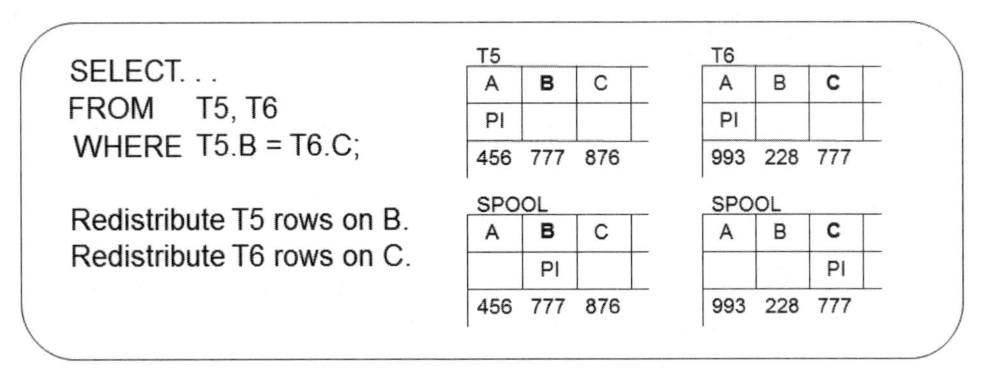

Figure 8.4

Join Strategies: Merge Strategy #4

Before two rows can be joined, they must be on the same AMP.

A RowKey join includes the row's partition number as well as its Row Hash. As for single-level partitioning, a Rowkey-Based Merge Join for multilevel partitioning requires equality conditions on all the primary index columns and partitioning columns of the two relations.

To be eligible for a RowKey-Based Merge Join, both relations must have the same partitioning. Otherwise, one of the relations must be spooled and partitioned to impose equal partitioning between the two.

Nested Join

Nested Joins are the best choice for OLTP applications. To invoke a Nested Join, the Optimizer must have:

- An equality value for a unique index (UPI or USI) on Table1.
- An equijoin on a column of that single row to any index on Table2.

With a Nested Join, the system retrieves the single row from Table1 and hashes the join column value to access matching Table2 row(s). The following diagram shows the various combinations of a nested join:

	T1	T2		
data value ⟶	UPI , data column ⟶	PI	= 2 AMPs	1 OR MORE ROWS RETURNED
data value ⟶	USI , data column ⟶	PI	= 3 AMPs	1 OR MORE ROWS RETURNED
data value ⟶	UPI , data column ⟶	USI	= 3 AMPs	1 ROW RETURNED
data value ⟶	USI , data column ⟶	USI	= 4 AMPs	1 ROW RETURNED
data value ⟶	UPI , data column ⟶	NUSI	= ALL AMPs	1 OR MORE ROWS RETURNED
data value ⟶	USI , data column ⟶	NUSI	= ALL AMPs	1 OR MORE ROWS RETURNED

Figure 8.5

Hash Join

Hash join is a method that performs better than merge join under certain conditions. Hash join is applicable *only* to equijoins. The performance enhancements gained with the dynamic hash join comes mainly from eliminating the need to sort the tables to be joined before performing the actual join operation.

The following chart shows how Teradata Database can use the various forms of the hash join to handle the following join types.

	HASH JOIN FORM		
HASH JOIN TYPE	CLASSIC	DYNAMIC HASH JOIN	DYNAMIC HASH JOIN WITH DYNAMIC ROW PARTITION ELIMINATION
Inner Hash Join	Yes	Yes	Yes
Left Outer Hash Join	Yes	Yes	No
Right Outer Hash Join	Yes	Yes	No
Full Outer Hash Join	Yes	Yes	No
Hash Inclusion Semijoin	No	Yes	Yes
Hash Exclusion Semijoin	No	Yes	Yes

Figure 8.6

Hash joins, like other join methods, perform optimally when the statistics on the join columns are current. This is particularly important for hash join costing to assist the Optimizer in detecting skew in the data. The Optimizer evaluates the relative costs of available join methods to determine the least expensive method of joining two tables.

If the small table is small enough to fit into one hash partition and it is being duplicated to all AMPs, the redistribution of the large table can be eliminated by this type of dynamic hash join. In such a case, the large table is read directly, without spooling, redistributing or sorting, and the hash join is performed between the small table spool and the large table.

Dynamic hash join provides the ability to do an equality join directly between a small table and a large table on non-primary index columns without placing the large table into a spool file. For dynamic hash join to be used, the left table must be small enough to fit in a single hash join partition.

Dynamic hash join can be used only when two tables are joined based on non-primary index columns, and one table, referred to as the left table, is very small compared to the other.

The dynamic hash join can be applied to left, right, and full outer joins as well as inner joins, and can also take advantage of equality conditions for dynamic partition elimination. The inclusion hash join and the exclusion hash join can also use dynamic partition elimination when you specify an equality condition.

If the small table won't fit into a single memory segment (partition), the rows will be hashed to a specific partition based upon an algorithm. They will then be sorted (in spool) into partition and hash code sequence.

The large table will then undergo a similar hash and sort.

When both tables have been hashed and sorted, the first partition of each side is read, and the hash join process takes place. When all of the rows from the large table partition have been compared to the small table partition rows, the next partition from both sides is read and the process repeats.

Exclusion Join

Exclusion joins are used to find rows that DON'T have a match. They may be implemented as merge or product joins. They are caused in NOT IN subqueries and EXCEPT operations.

They use 3-value logic (= , <> , unknown) on nullable columns.

- Define NOT IN columns as NOT NULL on the CREATE TABLE if possible.
- Use WHERE colname IS NOT NULL, or COALESCE (colname, 0) in queries against nullable join columns.

Product Joins

This is the most general form of a join. Any join type can be performed as a Product Join. It identifies the Small Table and duplicates it in spool on all AMPs. It does not sort the rows.

It compares every qualifying Table1 row to every qualifying Table2 row. Those that match the WHERE condition are saved in spool. It identifies the small table and may decide to re-read blocks from the large table if the AMP memory size is exceeded. It is called a Product Join because:

Total Compares = # Qualified Table1 Rows * # Qualified Table2 Rows

The internal compares become very costly when there are more rows than AMP memory can hold at one time. Product joins are caused by inequality and ORed join conditions. The system can choose to do a Product join if it is less expensive than other choices.

Cartesian Product Join

A Cartesian Join is an unconstrained join. Every row of the left table will be joined to every row of the right table. Sometimes, DBAs will run multiple Cartesian Joins to load-test the system.

Chapter 8: Practice Questions

1. Which join plan does the Parser always choose for inequality and ORed join conditions?
    a. Merge
    b. Exclusion
    c. Nested
    d. ROWID
    e. Product

2. What is the only join that doesn't always use all of the AMPs?
    a. Exclusion
    b. Hash
    c. Merge
    d. Nested
    e. Product

3. Which of the following joins will take place if there are no join conditions?
    a. Hash
    b. Nested
    c. Merge
    d. Exclusion
    e. Cartesian

4. A Hash Join can eliminate duplicating and sorting the large table only if ________.
    a. the rows of the small table won't fit entirely into one hash partition
    b. the rows of the small table require multiple hash partitions
    c. the join condition is inequality
    d. statistics on the two tables are non-existent

Chapter Notes

Utilize this space for notes, key points to remember, diagrams, areas of further study, etc.

Chapter 9: Join Indexes

Certification Objectives

- ✓ Given a scenario, identify when to use STJIs.
- ✓ Given a scenario, identify when to use Multi-table Join Indexes.
- ✓ Given a scenario, identify when to use AJIs.

Before You Begin

You should be familiar with the following terms and concepts.

Terms	Key Concepts
Join Indexes	What are the different options
Single Table Join Index	Considerations for utilizing
Multi-Table Join Indexes	Best practices for implementation
Aggregate Join Indexes	Determine the benefits for query optimization

Basic types of Join Indexes

Basically, a Join Index is a persistent materialized view. It may be based on one or more tables or be defined with pre-aggregated information. In addition, a Join Index can cover a query by containing the requested base table(s) columns. Join Indexes also have the ability to do a partial cover of a query. This means that information can be obtained from a combination of the Join Index and base table in order to satisfy the query.

There are several types of Join Indexes and each have a unique role in enhancing the performance of queries without applying denormalization techniques. The Optimizer is responsible for accessing Join Indexes. Therefore, Join Indexes can be utilized to create persistent pre-join and summary tables. They do this while maintaining the ability to support a wide range of decision support and ad hoc queries. These indexes permit you to undertake a wide variety of physical denormalizations of the database without affecting the normalization of the logical and physical models. The following are the basic types of Join Indexes:

1. Single-Table Join Indexes (STJI)
2. Multi-Table Join Indexes (MTJI)
3. Aggregate Join Indexes (AJI)

Customer

Customer Number	Address	Phone Number
PK		
UPI		

Order

Order Number	Customer Number	Order Date
PK	FK	
UPI		

Part

Part Number	Price	Desc
PK		
UPI		

Order_Part

Part Number	Order Number	Quantity
PK		
	NUPI	

NORMALIZED MODEL TABLES

DENORMALIZED INDEXES

Single Table Index on Order

Order Number	Customer Number	Order Date
	NUPI	

Multi-Table Index on Customerr,Order, Order_Part, and Part

Customer Number	Order Date	Order Number	Part Number	Price	Quantity
NUPI					

Multi-Table Aggregate Index

Customer Number	Order Date	SUM(Order/ Part/Price)
NUPI		

Figure 9.1

Note: An STJI may have a Primary Index different than the base table.

When to Use a Join Index

Join Indexes are not suited for all applications and situations. The usefulness of a Join Index, like that of any other index, depends on the type of work it is designed to perform. The recommendation is to always prototype a Join Index in order to evaluate the benefits to the applications, along with the support required, before adding it to your production environment. In some cases, the overhead to maintain a Join Index can outweigh the benefit.

The following outlines where a Join Index could provide performance benefits:

- Frequent joins of large tables that result in a significant number of the rows being joined.
- Joins of tables with a high degree of frequency in which the same columns are repeatedly requested.
- Vertical partitioning where only a subset of data in a base table is frequently joined resulting in a redistribution of rows.
- The overhead in time and storage capacity to maintain and create a Join Index does not outweigh its retrieval benefits.

Join Index Considerations

When deciding on a Join Index strategy, the following should be considered before implementing:

1. BLOB or CLOB data types are not allowed in the definition of a Join Index

2. When defining a Join Index with an outer join, all columns of the outer table must be referenced in the select list of the Join Index. If they are not referenced, the system will return an error.

3. Perm Space — a Join Index is a table in Teradata and uses Perm space in order to materialize the result set.

4. Fallback Protection — Join Indexes can be configured with Fallback.

5. MultiLoad, FastLoad, and the Teradata Parallel Transporter (TPT) LOAD and UPDATE operators cannot be used to load data when base tables have a Join Index defined. The Join Index must be dropped and recreated after the table has been loaded. However, TPump and the TPT STREAM operator support Join Indexes because they are row based update utilities.

6. Archiving is permitted on a base table or database that has a Join Index defined. However, a restore will not automatically rebuild the Join Index. Instead, the Join Index is marked as invalid and will have to be dropped and recreated manually.

7. Permanent journal to recover a base table with a Join Index defined is permitted. Keep in mind that the Join Index is not automatically rebuilt during the recovery process. Instead, the Join Index is marked as invalid and the Join Index must be dropped and recreated manually.

8. Statistics - It is recommended that statistics should be collected on the primary index and secondary indexes of the Join Index. This will give the Optimizer the ability choose the best path to complete the query.

Join Indexes versus Other Options

In Chapter 7, we discussed various denormalization techniques. Remember, the goal is to leave the base tables fully normalized and to create other solutions. The following topics compare Join Indexes against views, summary tables, and temporary tables.

Join Indexes versus Views

Join Index	View
Rows are physically stored on the disks	Rows are compiled each time the view is referenced
Ability to have a Primary Index	Cannot have a Primary Index
Uses up Perm space	Uses only Spool space, while the query is being executed
Main function is to increase access speed to data	Main function is to manipulate how data is seen in reports, and for security
Rows are not accessible to users	Rows are accessible to users with the proper rights

Figure 9.2

Join Indexes versus Summary Tables

Join Index	Summary Tables
Rows are physically stored on the disks	Rows are physically stored on the disks
Ability to have a Primary Index	Ability to have Primary Index
Uses up Perm space	Uses up Perm Space
Main function is to increase access speed to data – maintained by RDBMS	Main function is to increase access speed to data – users have to maintain
Rows are not accessible to users	Rows are accessible to users with the proper rights

Figure 9.3

Join Indexes versus Temporary Tables

Join Index	Temporary Tables
Rows are physically stored on the disks	Rows are in Spool or Temp space
Ability to have a Primary Index	Ability to have Primary Index
Uses up Perm space	Does not use Perm Space
Main function is to increase access speed to data	Main function is to allow for a quick and disposable look at the data
Rows are not accessible to users	Rows are accessible to users with the proper rights

Figure 9.4

Single-Table Join Index

Single-Table Join Indexes are one of the most useful constructs for tactical queries. The real benefit is that you are allowed to partition all or a subset of a very large base table as a "join index" on a different primary index than that used by the original base table. This is done in order to hash its rows to the same AMPs as another very large base table that it is frequently joined to.

The following figure shows a Single-Table Join Index (STJI) built on the Order table, but with its Primary Index based on the Customer_Number column.

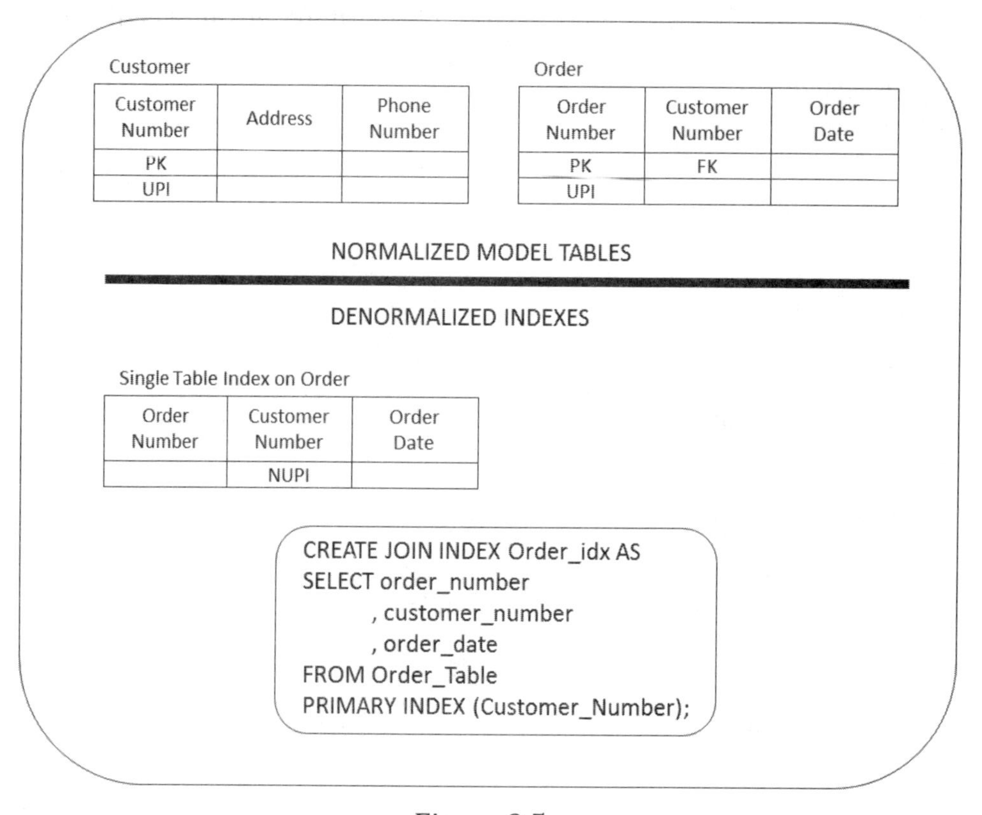

Figure 9.5

If a user queries the Order table with an equality condition on Order_Number, the system can use the base table's UPI for access. If the user queries the Order table with an equality condition on Customer_Number, the system can use the NUPI of the index for access. If the user does a join between the Customer and Order tables, the rows of the index are already on the same AMP as the Customer rows, so the system can do a PI to PI join.

Multi-Table Join Index

A multi-table Join Index is defined as creating a Join Index that involves more than one table, generally for joins of known queries. The essence behind a multi-table Join Index is that Teradata stores an answer set of an often-used query on disk. For example, Join Indexes for an outer join have the ability to preserve the unmatched rows resulting from the join. This is beneficial because this allows the Join Index to optimize more queries that have few join conditions. An example of a Covered Query is when all columns required by a query are available via a Join Index.

The following diagram shows a three-table Join Index.

Customer

Customer Number	Address	Phone Number
PK		
UPI		

Order

Order Number	Customer Number	Order Date
PK	FK	
UPI		

Part

Part Number	Price	Desc
PK		
UPI		

Order_Part

Part Number	Order Number	Quantity
PK		
	NUPI	

NORMALIZED MODEL TABLES

DENORMALIZED INDEXES

Multi-Table Index on Order, Order_Part, and Part

Customer Number	Order Date	Order Number	Part Number	Price	Quantity
NUPI					

```
CREATE JOIN INDEX  Order_Part_idx AS
SELECT  Customer_Number
           , Order_Date
           , Order_Number
           , Part_Number
           , Price
           , Quantity
FROM Order JOIN Order_Part
ON Order.Order_Number = Order_Part.Order_Number
JOIN Part
ON Order_Part.Part_Number = Part.Part_Number
Primary Index (Customer_Number);
```

Figure 9.6

Aggregate Join Index

If an application consistently accesses the same table with data aggregation, then an aggregate Join Index can offer some performance benefits. Keep in mind the following when implementing an Aggregate Join Index:

- Only sums and counts may be used in an Aggregate Join Index.
- All aggregations columns defined in the select list must include an "as" alias.
- The DISTINCT command is not permitted.
- COUNT and SUM columns should be defined as type FLOAT to avoid overflow.

The next diagram shows creating an aggregate index.

Customer

Customer Number	Address	Phone Number
PK		
UPI		

Order

Order Number	Customer Number	Order Date
PK	FK	
UPI		

Part

Part Number	Price	Desc
PK		
UPI		

Order_Part

Part Number	Order Number	Quantity
PK		
	NUPI	

NORMALIZED MODEL TABLES

DENORMALIZED INDEXES

Multi-Table Aggregate Index

Customer Number	Order Date	SUM(Order/ Part/Price)
NUPI		

```
CREATE JOIN INDEX Agg_Order_idx AS
SELECT  Customer_Number
, EXTRACT (MONTH FROM Order_Date AS Order_Month
, SUM( Part.Price * Order_Part.Quantity)  (DEC (6,2)) AS Order_Total
FROM Order JOIN Order_Part
ON Order.Order_Number = Order_Part.Order_Number
JOIN Part
ON Order_Part.Part_Number = Part.Part_Number
GROUP BY 1, 2
PRIMARY INDEX ( Customer_Number) ;
```

Figure 9.7

Sparse Index

The Sparse Join Index feature is a particularly useful variation of a Join Index. A WHERE clause in the CREATE JOIN INDEX statement limits the rows from the base table that will participate in the sparse Join Index, making a smaller and often quicker to build structure. Any Join Index, whether simple or aggregate, multi-table or single-table, can be sparse.

Sparse Indexes, like other index choices, should be chosen to support high frequency queries that require short response times. Typically Sparse Join Indexes provide the following benefits:

- Reduces the storage requirements for a Join Index.
- Makes access faster since the size of the JI is smaller.
- Use only a portion of the columns in the base table.
- Index only the values you want to index.
- Ignore some columns, e.g., nulls, to keep access smaller and faster than before.
- Avoid maintenance costs for updates.

Most Sparse Join Indexes are limited by date as shown below:

```
CREATE JOIN INDEX Order_2011 AS
SELECT Order_Number
       , Customer_Number
       , Order_Date
FROM Order
WHERE EXTRACT(YEAR FROM Order_Date) = 2011
PRIMARY INDEX(Customer_Number) ;
```

Figure 9.8

Sparse indexes, such as the above example, have good performance when it comes to join performance, along with updating the base table, because of the smaller subset of data being utilized for the sparse index, as illustrated below:

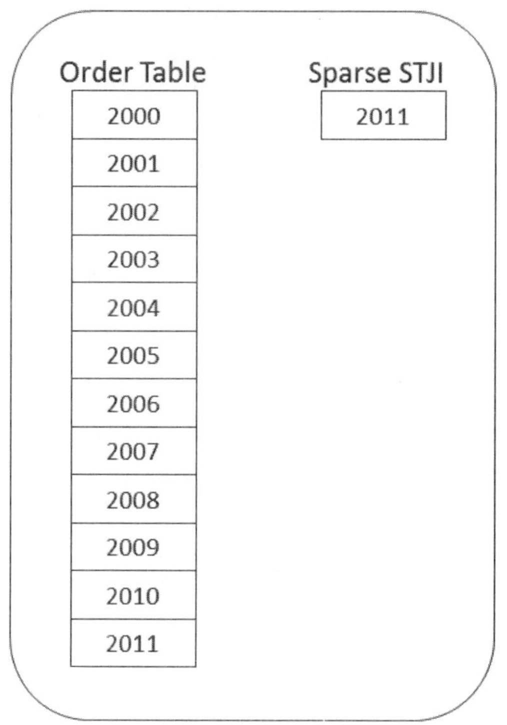

Figure 9.9

Global Join Index

Suppose there is a large table that needs to be joined frequently with another table on a column that is not the distributing column of the table. You can define a join index that redistributes the base table by the join column. However, because of the large number of rows and columns that need to be projected into the join index, the extra disk storage required does not allow the creation of such a join index.

You can define a join index in such a way that its partial coverage of a query can be extended further by joining with a parent base table to pick up any columns requested by the query but not referenced in the join index definition.

Such a join index, sometimes called a Global Index or Global Join Index (GJI), is defined with one of the following elements, which the Optimizer can use to join it with a parent base table to extend its coverage:

- One of the columns in the index definition is the keyword ROWID.
- The column set defining the UPI of the underlying base table.
- The column set defining a USI on the underlying base table.

A Global Join Index is basically a Join Index that contains a direct link to the base table rows. When you include the Row ID in a Join Index, the Row ID (Part # + Row Hash + Uniqueness Value) is stored. Global Indexes provide the following:

- Improved performance for certain classes of queries.
- Can provide reduced duplication of all the columns required to cover the queries resulting in better performance.
- Improved scalability for certain classes of queries.

Partial–Covering Global Join Indexes can provide:

- Can provide a single-table or a set of joined tables that has an access path to a base table.
- Each Index row points back to the real base row in the real base table.
- Will have rows hashed to a different AMP than the rows of the base table.
- Is very similar to a hashed NUSI but most likely won't access all the AMPs.

- Is also similar to a hashed USI, but most likely will be more than a 2-AMP operation.
- ODS (Operational Data Store) or tactical queries that involve an equality condition on a fairly unique column can use a global index which will change:
    - Table-level locks to row hash locks
    - All-AMP steps to group-AMP steps

Global Join Index - Multi-Table Join Back

Join back simply means that the ROWID is carried as part of the Join Index. This permits the index to "join back" to the base row, much like a NUSI does. It is one of the features of Partial-Covering Join Indexes. The following illustrates this feature:

```
CREATE JOIN INDEX CustOrdGlobal_IDX AS
SELECT c.customer_number
, c.ROWID AS Cust_Rowid
, c.Address
, c.Phone
, o.Order_Number
, o.ROWID AS Order_Rowid
, o.Order_Date
FROM Customer AS c JOIN Order AS o
ON c.Customer_Number = o.Customer_Number
PRIMARY INDEX(c.Customer_Number) ;
```

Figure 9.10

The total number of columns that you can use in Global Join Index is 64. If the number of columns in both tables is more than 64, the recommendation is to only include the most frequently referenced columns from each table. Another reason to only include a subset of columns is to minimize the size of the Join Index.

In this case, the Join Index subtable row will also include the Row ID of the base table row for the Customer table and the Row ID of the base table for the Orders table. The optimizer may choose to use the Join Index to get most of the data and join back to either the Customer or the Orders table to get additional requested data.

Starting with V2R5, the optimizer can build execution plans that can join back to either table. The terminology used in EXPLAIN plans that indicates a join back is "... using a row id join ...".

Global Join Index as a "Hashed-NUSI"

Global Join Index (GJI) on a single table is known as a Hashed NUSI. Keep in mind that typical NUSI is an all AMPs operation; however, GJI only accesses the AMPs that have rows it requires based on the SQL statement. From there, the GJI will use the Row IDs in this subtable to access only those AMPs that have rows.

Utilizing a global index in this situation is similar to a single-table Join Indexes with one clear distinction, which is the GJI carries the RowID back to the base table, and is used as an alternative means to get to the base table rows.

A "Hashed NUSI" global index also combines the best of a NUSI, which supports duplicate values, and a USI, which is hash-distributed on the indexed value which provides the ability to conduct group AMP processing. As discussed throughout this chapter, Global Join Indexes are transparent to the query and its use will be determined solely by the optimizer.

The true value of the GJI hashed NUSI is for situations where your result set is small and you want to avoid an all AMP operation that a NUSI always requires. This may not have a performance impact for systems that are small in size. However, for very large systems, with hundreds of AMPs, a group AMP operation that engages a small percentage of AMPs with this tactic could increase overall throughput as well as faster query response times.

Hash Indexes

Hash Indexes are very similar to both single-table join and Secondary Indexes. From an architectural standpoint, Hash Indexes incorporate the use of auxiliary structures that are transparently embedded in the Hash Index column. These auxiliary structures are components of the base table, and are added to the Hash Index definition, by default. This process distinctly distinguishes Hash Indexes from single-table Join Indexes.

Hash Indexes are similar to secondary indexes in the following ways:

- Created for a single table only.
- The CREATE syntax is simple and very similar to a Secondary Index.
- May cover a query without access of the base table rows.

Hash Indexes are like Join Indexes in the following ways:

- They "pre-locate" joinable rows to a common location.
- The distribution and sequencing of the rows is user specified.
- Very similar to single-table Join Index.
- A table with a trigger cannot also have a Join Index or a Hash Index.

Hash Indexes are unlike Join Indexes in the following ways:

- No aggregation operators are permitted.
- They are always defined on a single table.
- No secondary indexes may be built on the Hash Index.
- Automatically contains base table PI value as part of Hash Index subtable row.

When queries contain columns referenced and defined in Hash Index, then this will enable the Optimizer to cover the query rather than access its underlying base table.

It is worth noting that query covering can be accomplished by Secondary Indexes as well, but a Hash Index is better when there is a requirement for a wider range of query processing. However, because Hash Indexes have more overhead than Secondary Indexes, the recommendation is not to define them on a table when a Secondary Index would serve the same intention.

Hash Indexes Versus Single-Table Join Indexes

The reasons for using hash indexes are similar to those for using single-table join indexes. Not only can hash indexes optionally be specified to be distributed in such a way that their rows are AMP-local with their associated base table rows, they can also provide a transparent direct access path to those base table rows to complete a query only partially covered by the index.

This facility makes hash indexes somewhat similar to secondary indexes in function. Hash indexes are also useful for covering queries so that the base table need not be accessed at all. The most apparent external difference between hash and single-table join indexes is in the syntax of the SQL statements used to create them. The syntax for CREATE HASH INDEX is similar to that for CREATE INDEX. As a result, it is simpler to create a hash index than to create a functionally comparable single-table join index.

The following list summarizes the similarities of hash and single-table join indexes.

- Primary function of both is to improve query performance.
- Both are maintained automatically by the system when the relevant columns of their base table are updated by a DELETE, INSERT, or UPDATE statement.
- Both can be the object of any of the following SQL statements.
    - COLLECT STATISTICS (Optimizer Form)
    - DROP STATISTICS (Optimizer Form)
    - HELP INDEX
- Both receive their space allocation from permanent space and are stored in distinct tables.
- Both can be hash- and value-ordered
- Both can be compressed.
- Both can be FALLBACK protected.
- Neither can be queried or directly updated.
- Neither can store an arbitrary query result.
- Neither can be used to partially cover a query that contains a TOP *n* or TOP *m* PERCENT clause.
- Neither can be defined using the system-derived PARTITION column.
- Both share the same restrictions for use with the MultiLoad, FastLoad, TPT, and Archive/Recovery utilities.

The following table summarizes the differences between hash and join indexes:

HASH INDEX	JOIN INDEX
Indexes one table only	Can index multiple tables
A logical row corresponds to one and only one row in its referenced base table	A logical row can correspond to either of the following, depending on how the join index is defined: • One and only one row in the referenced base table • Multiple rows in the referenced base tables
Column list cannot contain aggregate or ordered analytical functions	Column list can contain aggregate functions
Cannot have a secondary index	Can have a secondary index
Supports transparently added, system-defined columns that point to the underlying base table rows	Does not add underlying base table row pointers implicitly Pointers to underlying base table rows can be created explicitly by defining one element of the column list using the keyword ROWID
Primary index cannot be partitioned	Primary index of non-compressed forms can be partitioned
Cannot be defined on a table that also has triggers	Can be defined on a table that also has triggers
Compression, if used, is added transparently by the system with no user input	Compression, if used, is explicitly specified in the CREATE JOIN INDEX request by the user

Figure 9.11

Chapter 9: Practice Questions

1. What type of Join Index will not be created by the following code?

```
CREATE JOIN INDEX Join_Indx AS
SELECT  Customer_Number
, EXTRACT (MONTH FROM Order_Date) AS Order_Month
, SUM( Part.Price * Order_Part.Quantity)  (DEC (6,2)) AS
Order_Total
FROM Order JOIN Order_Part
ON Order.Order_Number = Order_Part.Order_Number
JOIN Part
ON Order_Part.Part_Number = Part.Part_Number
WHERE EXTRACT(MONTH FROM Order_Date) = 2011
GROUP BY 1, 2
PRIMARY INDEX ( Customer_Number) ;
```

   a. Aggregate Join Index
   b. Multi-Table Join Index
   c. Sparse Join Index
   d. Single Table Join Index

2. Which of the following can be run against a table with a Join Index defined? (Choose 2)
   a. Recover
   b. FastLoad
   c. TPT Update
   d. MultiLoad
   e. Restore

3. Given these two tables, which of the following will create single table non-aggregate join index? (Choose 2)

```
CREATE TABLE employee_table
(Employee_No INTEGER NOT NULL
,Dept_No SMALLINT
,Mgr_employee_no INTEGER
,Last_name CHAR(20)
,First_name VARCHAR(12)
,Salary DECIMAL(8,2))
UNIQUE PRIMARY INDEX (Employee_No)
INDEX (Last_name)
INDEX (Dept_No);

CREATE TABLE department_table
(Dept_No SMALLINT NOT NULL
,Department_name CHAR(20)
,Mgr_No INTEGER
,Budget DECIMAL(10,2))
UNIQUE PRIMARY INDEX (Dept_No)
INDEX (Department_name)
INDEX (Mgr_No);
```

a. CREATE JOIN INDEX indx_1 AS
   SELECT employee_no, dept_no, mgr_employee_no, last_name,first_name, salary
   FROM employee_table
   PRIMARY INDEX (mgr_employee_no);
b. CREATE JOIN INDEX indx_2 AS
   SELECT employee_no, last_name, first_name, e.dept_no, department_name
   FROM employee_table AS e JOIN department_table AS d
   ON e.dept_no = d.dept_no;

c. CREATE JOIN INDEX indx_3 AS
SELECT d.dept_no, department_name, budget, SUM(salary) AS tot_sal
FROM department_table AS d
JOIN employee_table AS e
ON d.dept_no = e.dept_no
GROUP BY 1,2,3;

d. CREATE JOIN INDEX indx_4 AS
SELECT *
FROM employee_table
PRIMARY INDEX (dept_no);

e. CREATE JOIN INDEX indx_5 AS
SELECT dept_no, SUM(salary) AS tot_sal
FROM employee_table
GROUP BY 1;

4. Given these two tables, which of the following will create a non-aggregate multi-table join index?

```
CREATE TABLE employee_table
(Employee_No INTEGER NOT NULL
,Dept_No SMALLINT
,Mgr_employee_no INTEGER
,Last_name CHAR(20)
,First_name VARCHAR(12)
,Salary DECIMAL(8,2))
UNIQUE PRIMARY INDEX (Employee_No)
INDEX (Last_name)
INDEX (Dept_No);

CREATE TABLE department_table
(Dept_No SMALLINT NOT NULL
,Department_name CHAR(20)
,Mgr_No INTEGER
,Budget DECIMAL(10,2))
UNIQUE PRIMARY INDEX (Dept_No)
INDEX (Department_name)
INDEX (Mgr_No);
```

   a. CREATE JOIN INDEX indx_1 AS
      SELECT employee_no, dept_no, mgr_employee_no, last_name,first_name, salary
      FROM employee_table
      PRIMARY INDEX (mgr_employee_no);
   b. CREATE JOIN INDEX indx_2 AS
      SELECT employee_no, last_name, first_name, e.dept_no, department_name
      FROM employee_table AS e JOIN department_table AS d
      ON e.dept_no = d.dept_no;
   c. CREATE JOIN INDEX indx_3 AS

```
SELECT d.dept_no, department_name, budget,
SUM(salary) AS tot_sal
FROM department_table AS d
JOIN employee_table AS e
ON d.dept_no = e.dept_no
GROUP BY 1,2,3;
```

d. CREATE JOIN INDEX indx_4 AS
```
SELECT *
FROM employee_table
PRIMARY INDEX (dept_no);
```

e. CREATE JOIN INDEX indx_5 AS
```
SELECT dept_no, SUM(salary) AS tot_sal
FROM employee_table
GROUP BY 1;
```

5. Given these two tables, which of the following will create multi-table AJI?

```
CREATE TABLE employee_table
(Employee_No INTEGER NOT NULL
,Dept_No SMALLINT
,Mgr_employee_no INTEGER
,Last_name CHAR(20)
,First_name VARCHAR(12)
,Salary DECIMAL(8,2))
UNIQUE PRIMARY INDEX (Employee_No)
INDEX (Last_name)
INDEX (Dept_No);

CREATE TABLE department_table
(Dept_No SMALLINT NOT NULL
,Department_name CHAR(20)
,Mgr_No INTEGER
,Budget DECIMAL(10,2))
UNIQUE PRIMARY INDEX (Dept_No)
INDEX (Department_name)
INDEX (Mgr_No);
```

a. CREATE JOIN INDEX indx_1 AS
   SELECT employee_no, dept_no, mgr_employee_no, last_name,first_name, salary
   FROM employee_table
   PRIMARY INDEX (mgr_employee_no);
b. CREATE JOIN INDEX indx_2 AS
   SELECT employee_no, last_name, first_name, e.dept_no, department_name
   FROM employee_table AS e JOIN department_table AS d
   ON e.dept_no = d.dept_no;

c. CREATE JOIN INDEX indx_3 AS
   SELECT d.dept_no, department_name, budget, SUM(salary) AS tot_sal
   FROM department_table AS d
   JOIN employee_table AS e
   ON d.dept_no = e.dept_no
   GROUP BY 1,2,3;
d. CREATE JOIN INDEX indx_4 AS
   SELECT *
   FROM employee_table
   PRIMARY INDEX (dept_no);
e. CREATE JOIN INDEX indx_5 AS
   SELECT dept_no, SUM(salary) AS tot_sal
   FROM employee_table
   GROUP BY 1;

6. Given these two tables, which of the following will create a single table AJI?

```
CREATE TABLE employee_table
(Employee_No INTEGER NOT NULL
,Dept_No SMALLINT
,Mgr_employee_no INTEGER
,Last_name CHAR(20)
,First_name VARCHAR(12)
,Salary DECIMAL(8,2))
UNIQUE PRIMARY INDEX (Employee_No)
INDEX (Last_name)
INDEX (Dept_No);

CREATE TABLE department_table
(Dept_No SMALLINT NOT NULL
,Department_name CHAR(20)
,Mgr_No INTEGER
,Budget DECIMAL(10,2))
UNIQUE PRIMARY INDEX (Dept_No)
INDEX (Department_name)
INDEX (Mgr_No);
```

a. CREATE JOIN INDEX indx_1 AS
   SELECT employee_no, dept_no, mgr_employee_no, last_name,first_name, salary
   FROM employee_table
   PRIMARY INDEX (mgr_employee_no);
b. CREATE JOIN INDEX indx_2 AS
   SELECT employee_no, last_name, first_name, e.dept_no, department_name
   FROM employee_table AS e JOIN department_table AS d
   ON e.dept_no = d.dept_no;

c. CREATE JOIN INDEX indx_3 AS
   SELECT d.dept_no, department_name, budget, SUM(salary) AS tot_sal
   FROM department_table AS d
   JOIN employee_table AS e
   ON d.dept_no = e.dept_no
   GROUP BY 1,2,3;
d. CREATE JOIN INDEX indx_4 AS
   SELECT *
   FROM employee_table
   PRIMARY INDEX (dept_no);
e. CREATE JOIN INDEX indx_5 AS
   SELECT dept_no, SUM(salary) AS tot_sal
   FROM employee_table
   GROUP BY 1;

Chapter Notes

Utilize this space for notes, key points to remember, diagrams, areas of further study, etc.

Chapter 10: Explains

Certification Objectives

- ✓ Interpret the EXPLAIN syntax.
- ✓ Interpret the EXPLAINs of Joins.

Before You Begin

You should be familiar with the following terms and concepts.

Terms	Key Concepts
Row Hash Match	How does this get utilized
Single AMP Operations	What is done to complete this operation
Inclusion Join	Explain how this is implemented
Merge Join	What join type will create this

Explain Terminology

Most EXPLAIN text is easy to understand. The following additional definitions may be helpful:

... (Last Use) ...

- A spool file is no longer needed and will be released when this step completes.

... with no residual conditions ...

- All applicable conditions have been applied to the rows.

... END TRANSACTION ...

- Transaction locks are released, and changes are committed.

... eliminating duplicate rows ...

- Performs a DISTINCT operation (Duplicate rows only exist in spool files and MULTI-SET tables)

... by way of the sort key in spool field1 ...

- Field1 is created to allow a tag sort.

... we do an ABORT test ...

- Caused by an ABORT or ROLLBACK statement.

... by way of a traversal of index #n extracting row ids only ...

- A spool file is built containing the Row IDs found in a secondary index (index #n) for qualifying rows.

... we do a SMS (set manipulation step) ...

- Combining rows using a UNION, EXCEPT, or INTERSECT operator.

... we do a BMSMS (bit map set manipulation step)

- Doing a NUSI Bit Map operation.

... which is redistributed by hash code to all AMPs.
... which is duplicated on all AMPs.

- Relocating data in preparation for a join.

... (one_AMP) or (group_AMPs)

- Indicates one AMP or a subset of AMPs will be used instead of all AMPs.

... ("NOT (table_name.column_name IS NULL)")

- Feature in which the optimizer realizes that the column being joined to is NOT NULL or has referential integrity.

... Joined using a row id join ...

- Indicates a join back condition with a join index.

Full Table Scan

The following Explain shows a full-table scan:

```
EXPLAIN SELECT * FROM employee_table;
```

Figure 10.1

```
   First, we lock a distinct CSQL_CLASS."pseudo table"
   for read on a Row Hash to prevent global deadlock for
   CSQL_CLASS.employee_table
2) Next, we lock CSQL_CLASS.employee_table for read
3) We do an all-AMPs RETRIEVE step from
   CSQL_CLASS.employee_table by way of an all-rows scan
   with no residual conditions into Spool 1 (group_amps),
   which is built locally on the AMPs.  The size of Spool
   1 is estimated with low confidence to be 6 rows (546
```

```
   bytes).
   The estimated time for this step is 0.03 seconds.
4) Finally, we send out an END TRANSACTION step to all
   AMPs involved in processing the request.
-> The contents of Spool 1 are sent back to the user as
   the result of statement 1.  The total estimated time
   is 0.03 seconds.
```

Unique Primary Index (UPI)

The following is an Explain of a UPI retrieval:

```
EXPLAIN SELECT * FROM employee_table WHERE employee_no =
2000000;
```

Figure 10.2

```
1) First, we do a single-AMP RETRIEVE step from
   CSQL_CLASS.EMPLOYEE_TABLE by way of the unique primary
   index "CSQL_CLASS.EMPLOYEE_TABLE.Employee_No =
   2000000" with no residual conditions.  The estimated
   time for this step is 0.01 seconds.
-> The row is sent directly back to the user as the
   result of statement 1.  The total estimated time is
   0.01 seconds.
```

Non-Unique Primary Index (NUPI)

The following shows an Explain of a NUPI retrieval.

```
EXPLAIN SELECT * FROM emp_job_table WHERE job_no = 30010;
```

Figure 10.3

```
1) First, we do a single-AMP RETRIEVE step from
   CSQL_CLASS.EMP_job_table by way of the primary index
   "CSQL_CLASS.EMP_job_table.job_no = 30010" with no
   residual conditions into Spool 1 (one-amp), which is
   built locally on that AMP.  The size of Spool 1 is
```

```
   estimated with low confidence to be 2 rows (58 bytes).
   The estimated time for this step is 0.02 seconds.
-> The contents of Spool 1 are sent back to the user as
   the result of statement 1.  The total estimated time
   is 0.02 seconds.
```

Unique Secondary Index (USI)

The following is an Explain of a USI retrieval:

```
EXPLAIN SELECT * FROM emp_job_table WHERE job_no = 20010 AND
emp_no = 1121334;
```

Figure 10.4

```
1) First, we do a two-AMP RETRIEVE step from
   CSQL_CLASS.emp_job_table by way of unique index # 4
   "CSQL_CLASS.emp_job_table.job_no = 20010,
   CSQL_CLASS.emp_job_table.emp_no = 1121334" with no
   residual conditions.  The estimated time for this step
   is 0.01 seconds.
-> The row is sent directly back to the user as the
   result of statement 1.  The total estimated time is
   0.01 seconds.
```

Non-Unique Secondary Index (NUSI)

```
EXPLAIN SELECT * FROM STUDENT_TABLE WHERE class_code = 'FR';
```

Figure 10.5

```
1) First, we lock a distinct CSQL_CLASS."pseudo table"
   for read on a Row Hash to prevent global deadlock for
   CSQL_CLASS.student_table.
2) Next, we lock CSQL_CLASS.student_table for read.
3) We do an all-AMPs RETRIEVE step from
   CSQL_CLASS.student_table by way of index # 4
   "CSQL_CLASS.student_table.class_code = 'FR'with no
```

```
   residual conditions into Spool 1, which is built
   locally on the AMPs.  The size of Spool 1 is estimated
   with low confidence to be 2 rows (182 bytes).
   The estimated time for this step is 0.03 seconds.
4) Finally, we send out an END TRANSACTION step to all
   AMPs involved in processing the request.
-> The contents of Spool 1 are sent back to the user as
   the result of statement 1.  The total estimated time
   is 0.03 seconds.
```

Pseudo Locks

"Pseudo Table" Locks prevent two users from getting conflicting locks with all-AMP requests.

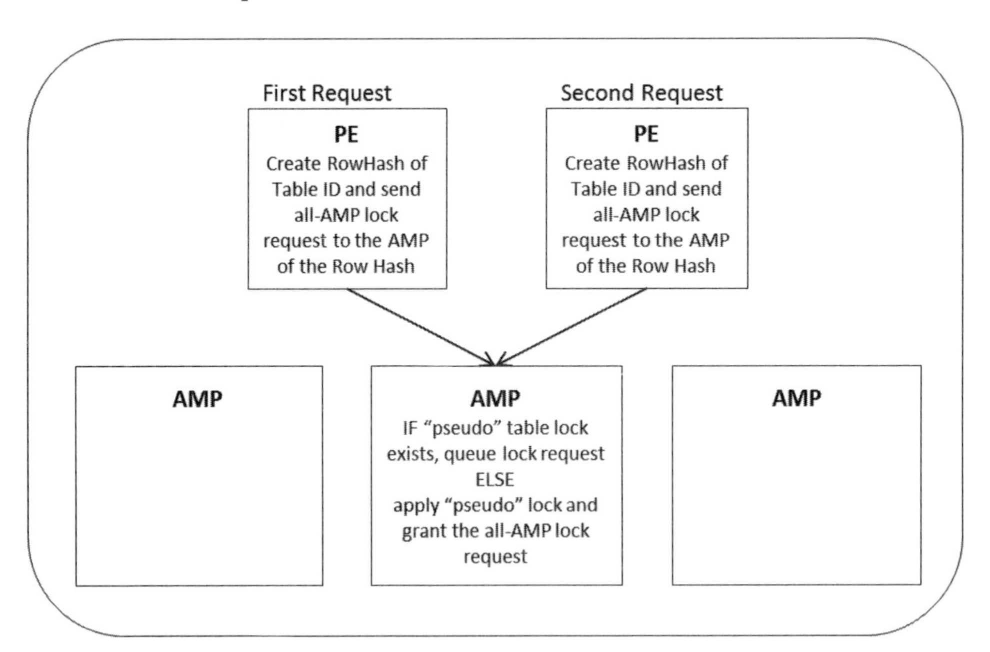

Figure 10.6

Confidence Levels

The EXPLAIN facility may express "confidence" for a retrieve from a table. Some of the phrases used are:

. . . with high confidence . . .

- Restricting conditions exist on index(es) or column(s) that have collected statistics.

. . . with low confidence . . .

- Restricting conditions exist on index(es) having no statistics, but estimates can be based upon a sampling of the index(es).
- Restricting conditions exist on index(es) or column(s) that have collected statistics but are "ANDed" together with conditions on non-indexed columns.
- Restricting conditions exist on index(es) or column(s) that have collected statistics but are "ORed" together with other conditions.

. . . with no confidence . . .

- Conditions outside the above.

The following are "confidence" phrases for a join:

. . . with index join confidence . . .

- A join condition via a primary index.

. . . with high confidence . . .

- One input relation has high confidence and the other has high or index join confidence.

. . . with low confidence . . .

- One input relation has low confidence and the other has low, high, or join index confidence.

. . . with no confidence . . .

- One input relation has no confidence.
- Statistics do not exist for either join field.

Query Cost Estimates

Row estimates:

- May be estimated using random samples, statistics or indexes.
- Are assigned a confidence level - high, low or none.
- Affect timing estimates - more rows, more time needed.

Timings:

- Used to determine the 'lowest cost' plan.
- Total cost generated if all processing steps have assigned cost.
- Not intended to predict wall-clock time, useful for comparisons.

Miscellaneous Notes:

- Estimates too large to display show 3 asterisks (***).
- The accuracy of the time estimate depends upon the accuracy of the row estimate.
- Low and no confidence may indicate a need to collect statistics on indexes or columns involved in restricting conditions.
- You may otherwise consider a closer examination of the conditions in the query for possible changes that may improve the confidence.

- Collecting statistics or altering the conditions has no real impact unless it influences the optimizer to pick a better plan.

Parallel Operations

PARALLEL STEPS are AMP steps that can execute concurrently:

- They have no functional overlap and do not contend for resources.
- They improve performance.
- The Optimizer generates PARALLEL STEPS whenever possible.
- EXPLAIN text identifies Parallel Steps.

The following diagram shows an example of parallel steps:

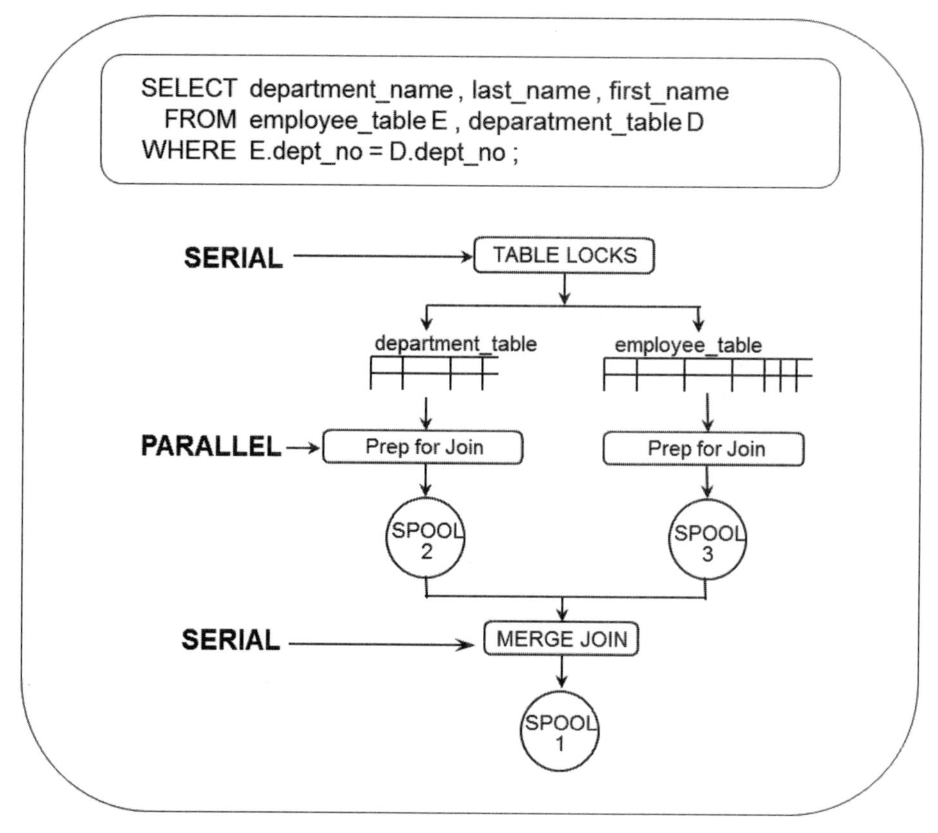

Figure 10.7

Redistributed by Hash Code

This means the system is moving row copies to put them on the same AMPs as the rows they are to be joined to. This is typically an example of doing a PI join to a non-PI column set.

Duplicated on All AMPs

This is another join preparation step. Each AMP sends copies of its qualifying rows and columns to all of the AMPs, which results in every AMP having a complete copy of the qualifying rows.

Join Index

If a Join Index exists, the Parser will use it if it's the least expensive solution. The following is an Explain where the Parser used the JI instead of accessing the underlying base tables.

```
SELECT o.order_date
       , COUNT (c.customer_id)
FROM customer_table c
INNER JOIN order_table o
ON c.customer_no = o.customer_no
WHERE o.order_date = '2008-08-18'
GROUP BY 1;
```

Figure 10.8

```
1) First, we lock CSQL_CLASS.customer_order_idx for read.
2) Next, we do a SUM step to aggregate from join index
   table CSQL_CLASS.customer_order_idx by way of an all-
   rows scan with a condition of
   "CSQL_CLASS.customer_order_idx.order_date = DATE '2008-
   08-18'"), and the grouping identifier in field 1.
   Aggregate Intermediate Results are computed globally,
   then placed in Spool 3. The size of Spool 3 is estimated
   with high confidence to be 1 rows.
3) We do an all-AMPs RETRIEVE step from Spool 3 (Last Use)
   by way of an all-rows scan into Spool 1, which is built
   locally on the AMPs. The size of Spool 1 is estimated
   with high confidence to be 1 row. The estimated time for
   this step is 0.17 seconds.
4) Finally, we send out an END TRANSACTION step to all AMPs
   involved in processing the request.
-> The contents of Spool 1 are sent back to the user as the
   result of statement 1. The total estimated time is 0.17
   seconds.
```

BMSMS Bit Mapping

BMSMS = Bit Map Set Manipulation Step = NUSI Bit Mapping. This is a processing step where the system combines multiple weakly selective equality NUSIs that are ANDed together to reduce the number of I/Os to the base table.

PPI Tables and Partitions

The following are phrases associated with PPI tables and their partitions:

"a single partition of" or "*n partitions of*"

- Indicates that an AMP or AMPs only need to access a single partition or *n partitions of a table.*
- Indicates *partition elimination occurred.*
- Partition elimination can occur for SELECTs, UPDATEs, and DELETEs.
- For a DELETE, Optimizer recognizes partitions in which all rows are deleted.
    - Rows in such partitions are deleted without using the transient journal.

"all partitions of"

- All partitions are accessed for primary index access in processing the query.

"SORT to partition Spool m by RowKey"

- The spool is to be sorted by rowkey (Partition and RowID).
- Partitioning the spool file in this way allows for a faster join with the partitioned table.

"a rowkey-based"

- The join is hash-based by partition (rowkey). In this case, there are equality constraints on both the partitioning and primary index columns.
- When this phrase is not reported, then the join is hash-based.

"enhanced by dynamic partition ..."

- Indicates a join condition where dynamic partition elimination has been used.

"of a single partition" or "of *n* partitions"

- The optimizer determined that all rows in a single partition, or *n* partitions, can be deleted. In some cases, this allows for faster deletion of the entire partition.

Group AMPs, SORT, Eliminating Duplicate Rows, and No Residual Conditions

(group_amps)

- The operation is a group AMP operation, meaning that it occurs on more than 1, but fewer than all, AMPs in the system.

Sort

- A sort operation occurs.

eliminating duplicate rows

- Duplicate rows can exist in spool files, either as a result of selection of nonunique columns from any table or of selection from a MULTISET table. This is a DISTINCT operation.

no residual conditions

- Means that no conditions outside a join or index access is applied.
- Rows are selected in their entirety; there are no specific search conditions.

Last Use, End Transaction, and Computed Globally

Here are some common Explain phrases:

(Last Use)

- This term identifies the last reference to a spool file that contains intermediate data that produces a statement's final result.
- The spool file is released following this step.

END TRANSACTION step

- This indicates that processing is complete and that any locks on the data may be released.
- Changes made by the transaction are committed.

computed globally

This describes a specific form of aggregation where the entire aggregate algorithm is applied instead of a "local aggregation" which is computed locally when the group columns reference the PI columns of a base table or spool.

Chapter 10: Practice Questions

1. Which phrase is associated with the system combining rows during a UNION?
    a. ... which is duplicated on all AMPs.
    b. ... we do a BMSMS (bit map set manipulation step)
    c. ... we do a SMS (set manipulation step)
    d. ... by way of the sort key in spool field1 ...

2. An END TRANSACTION step appears with which retrieval? (Choose 2)
    a. UPI
    b. NUPI
    c. USI
    d. NUSI
    e. FTS

3. Which "confidence" phrase indicates restricting conditions exist on index(es) or column(s) that have collected statistics?
    a. ... with no confidence ...
    b. ... with high confidence ...
    c. ... with no confidence ...
    d. ... with join index confidence ...

4. Which "confidence" phrase indicates restricting conditions exist on index(es) or column(s) that have collected statistics but are "ORed" together with other conditions?
    a. ... with no confidence ...
    b. ... with high confidence ...
    c. ... with low confidence ...
    d. ... with join index confidence ...

5. Which phrase indicates an intermediate spool file will be released?
    a. END TRANSACTION
    b. (last use)
    c. ... no residual conditions ...
    d. ... eliminating duplicate rows ...

Chapter Notes

Utilize this space for notes, key points to remember, diagrams, areas of further study, etc.

Chapter 11: Query Analysis and Tools

Certification Objectives

- ✓ Determine the methods to uncover embedded (nested) views.
- ✓ Explain partial value searches and data conversions on index utilization.
- ✓ Explain the effects of row access, selection, aggregation, and selectivity on query optimization.
- ✓ Identify table-level options that minimize table fragmentation.
- ✓ Identify the effects of conflicting implicit data type conversions.
- ✓ Identify the utilities available to perform Query Analysis.
- ✓ Interpret DBQL output.
- ✓ When performing a CREATE TABLE AS, identify possible skewing risks.

Before You Begin

You should be familiar with the following terms and concepts.

Terms	Key Concepts
DBQL	Considerations for utilization
PACKDISK	Explain how this works to free cylinders
Teradata Workload Analyzer	How to utilize for application analysis
Visual Explain	Query analysis and optimization
MERGEBLOCKRATIO	Combining smaller data blocks into larger data blocks

Help and Show Commands

Teradata Database SQL provides several powerful statements for system administrators, database and security administrators, and application programmers. The statements are HELP and SHOW.

The following is a list of the HELP commands:

HELP CAST
HELP COLUMN
HELP CONSTRAINT
HELP DATABASE
HELP USER
HELP ERROR TABLE
HELP FUNCTION
HELP HASH INDEX
HELP INDEX
HELP JOIN INDEX
HELP MACRO
HELP TABLE
HELP VIEW
HELP METHOD
HELP PROCEDURE
HELP REPLICATION GROUP
HELP SESSION
HELP STATISTICS
HELP TRANSFORM
HELP TRIGGER
HELP TYPE
HELP VOLATILE TABLE
HELP 'SQL'

The SHOW commands return the actual create text of the object:

SHOW CAST
SHOW ERROR TABLE
SHOW FUNCTION
SHOW HASH INDEX
SHOW JOIN INDEX
SHOW MACRO
SHOW METHOD
SHOW PROCEDURE
SHOW REPLICATION GROUP
SHOW TABLE
SHOW TRIGGER
SHOW TYPE
SHOW VIEW

Using DBQL

You can use DBQL to log query processing activity to:

- Capture query/statement counts and response times.
- Discover potential application improvements.
- Make further refinements to workload groupings and scheduling.
- Have SQL text and processing steps analyzed.

DBQL provides a series of predefined tables that can store historical records of queries and their duration, performance, and target activity based on rules you specify. DBQL is flexible enough to log information on the variety of SQL requests, from short transactions to longer-running analysis and mining queries. You begin and end collection for a user or group of users and/or one or a list of accounts.

In addition to being able to capture the entire SQL statement, DBQL also provides key insights into other aspects of a query such as whether it was aborted or delayed by Teradata DWM, the start and end time. DBQL operates asynchronously. As a result, the logging activity has a much lower impact on the overall response time of given transactions.

Furthermore, DBQL writes its information to internal memory buffers or caches. These are flushed to disk when the buffer is full, or at the time indicated by the DBS Control Record "DBQLFlushRate". The default rate is every 10 minutes, but the DBA can change the rate based on requirements.

DBC.Accesslog

DBC.AccessLog is a view on the Data Dictionary table DBC.AccLogTbl.

Each row displayed in the AccessLog is the result of a privilege check. Whether a privilege check is logged depends on the presence and the criteria of an access logging rule defined in AccLogRules.

In AccLogRules, each Access Rule column is named for a particular privilege, which is also associated with an access action and an SQL statement. In each column, each character position represents the frequency with which checks performed on that privilege are to be logged.

Entries in AccLogRules are created when the Security Administrator issues a BEGIN LOGGING command.

MERGEBLOCKRATIO

The MERGEBLOCKRATIO option provides a way to combine existing small data blocks into a single larger data block during full table modification operations. This is for permanent tables and permanent journal tables and is not available for volatile and global temporary tables. The file system uses the merge block ratio that you specify to reduce the number of data blocks within a table that would otherwise consist mainly of small data blocks. Reducing the number of small data blocks enables Teradata Database to reduce the I/O overhead of operations that must read and modify a large percentage of the table.

PACKDISK

The PACKDISK utility is a very expensive operation, and is run to free up cylinders of disk space, by compacting data, not spool, as shown in the following figure. Remember, a cylinder may contain data or spool, but not both.

There are steps you can take to reduce how often PACKDISK has to be run. Here are some suggestions:

- If you have a history table where you are adding and deleting rows, leave enough free space to add rows, plus a safety factor. For example, you capture 12 months of history before deleting the oldest month of data.
    - Add one month to twelve months: 1/13 = 7.7%
    - Add an additional half month as a safety factor: 1.5/13.5 = 11.1%
    - Or add an additional month as a safety factor: 2/14 = 14.3%
    - Set Free Space Percent in the range of 10-15%

- If you plan on adding rows to a table after it's been FastLoaded, be sure to provide enough free space for the additional rows.

The table header contains the FSP for each table. If you change the default FSP, the system uses the new default the next time you modify the table. FSP has no effect on block size. The action performed by PackDisk is shown in the following figure:

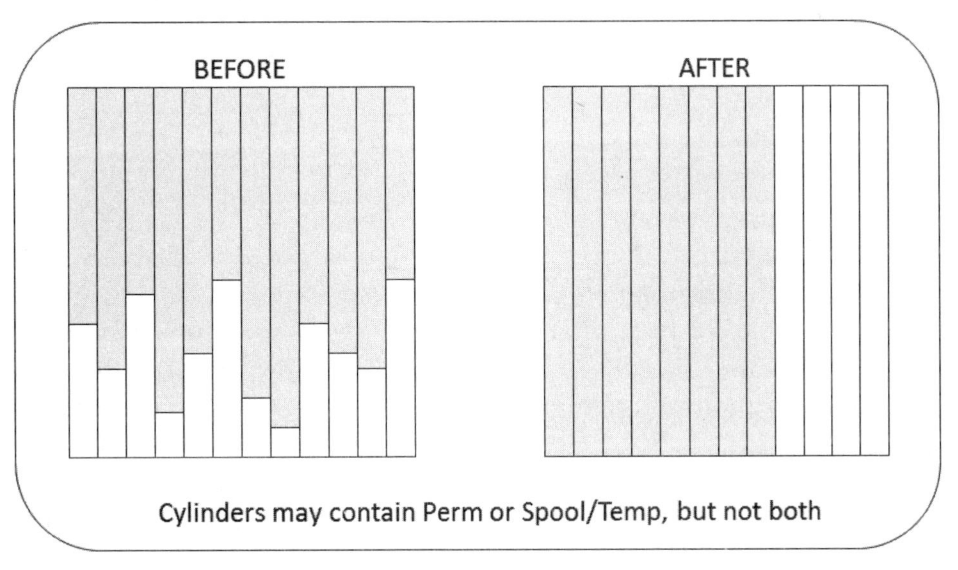

Figure 11.1

Teradata Index Wizard

Teradata Index Wizard analyzes SQL statements in a workload, using the contents of the tables in QCD, and recommends the best set of indexes to use.

Index Wizard helps re-engineer existing databases by recommending, for example, SI definitions that may improve the overall efficiency of the workload. Recommendations can include adding or deleting Secondary Indexes to an existing design.

Index Wizard creates workload statements, analyzes them, and then creates a series of reports and index recommendations that show various costs and statistics. The reports help you decide if the index recommendation is appropriate or not.

Index Wizard validates the index recommendations comparing performance between existing physical database design and recommended physical database design enhancements. Use these recommendations to evaluate potential performance improvements and modify the database accordingly.

Visual Explain

Teradata Visual Explain adds another dimension to the EXPLAIN modifier by visually depicting the execution plan of complex SQL statements in a simplified manner. It presents a graphical view of the statement broken down into discrete steps that show the flow of data during execution.

Skewed Distribution

Skewed distribution means that there are an uneven number of rows per AMP. This is generally caused by a poor choice of a NUPI. However, skewed distribution can also occur for a UPI table when the number of table rows is small relative to the number of AMPS is the system.

On full table scans, the AMPS with the fewer row will finish sooner and have to wait for the AMPS with the high number of rows. This results in poor CPU parallel efficiency.

Skewed distribution also results in increased I/O on updates and inserts to set tables and temporal tables for those rows having the same NUPI value, due to the need to do duplicate row checking, unless there is a USI on the table.

As an example, suppose you have a 1 billion row table with 10,000 rows having the same NUPI value. Every time you insert a row having that NUPI value, the system has to do 10,000 duplicate row checks. If an update program inserts 100 rows having that NUPI value, 1,000,000 duplicate row checks will have to be performed by that single AMP.

CREATE TABLE ... AS

If the source is a base table, the target table defaults to the source table kind unless you specify an explicit table kind.

If the source is a subquery, the session mode (ANSI, BTET) determines the table kind, unless you explicitly define the table kind.

The following general rules apply to table definitions copied using an AS clause in CREATE TABLE.

- When you use a subquery as your source definition, the standard defaults for the Primary Index will be used by the system. That means the first column will be a NUPI unless there is a PK or UNIQUE constraint defined. If you do not want the target table to have a Primary Index, you must state NO PRIMARY INDEX.
- When you have a subquery as your source, any target column that maps to a subquery expression will be assigned the data type of the expression result.

When you specify an existing table as the source table definition in the AS clause, then the new table always assumes the following table-level characteristics of the source table.

- Column structures, including columns with UDT, Period, ARRAY, and VARRAY types.
- Fallback options
- Journaling options
  - If the new table is a global temporary or volatile table, then permanent journaling is *not* copied
- All defined indexes except hash and join indexes.

If indexes are explicitly defined for the target table, then that table does *not* assume any source table indexes.

Keep in mind that primary index chosen for the target table may cause skewed distribution. Use the Hash Functions (HASHAMP, HASHBACKAMP, HASHBUCKET, HASHROW) to check for skew in advance.

Avoid Implicit Data Conversion

Normally, operands must be of the same data type to do a comparison. One of the powerful abilities of Teradata SQL is the ability to compare operands of different data types. If two operands are not of the same data type, Teradata will automatically convert one, or both, to a common data type and then do the comparison.

As an example, comparisons between character and numeric data types require that the character field be convertible to a numeric value. Avoid conversions like this in a WHERE clause.

Implicit conversions (implied CAST) are a Teradata extension to the ANSI SQL-2008 standard.

If operand data types differ, then the Teradata Database performs an implied CAST according to the following table in Figure 11.2.

IF one expression operand is ...	**AND the other expression operand is ...**	**THEN Teradata Databasse compares the data as ...**
Character	Character	Character
	Date	Date
	BYTEINT SMALLINT INTEGER FLOAT	FLOAT
	Period	Period
CHAR(k) VARCHAR(k) where k <= 16	BIGINT DECIMAL(m,n)	FLOAT The system returns an error for character data with GRAPHIC server character set.
CHAR(k)	DECIMAL(m,n)	FLOAT

VARCHAR(k) where k > 16	NUMBER where m <= 16	The system returns an error for character data with GRAPHIC server character set.
	BIGINT DECIMAL(m,n) NUMBER where m > 16	The system returns an error.
BYTEINT	SMALLINT	SMALLINT
BYTEINT SMALLINT	INTEGER	INTEGER
BYTEINT SMALLINT INTEGER BIGINT	BIGINT	BIGINT
BYTEINT	DECIMAL(m,n) where m = 18 and m-n >=3	DECIMAL(18,n)
SMALLINT	DECIMAL(m,n) where m <= 18 and m-n >= 5	
INTEGER	DECIMAL(m,n) where m <= 18 and m-n >= 10	
DATE		
BYTEINT	DECIMAL(m,n) where m > 18 or m-n <3	DECIMAL(38,n)
SMALLINT	DECIMAL(m,n)	

	where m > 18 or m-n < 5	
INTEGER	DECIMAL(m,n) where m > 18 or m-n < 10	
DATE		
BIGINT	DECIMAL(m,n)	

DECIMAL(m,n)	DECIMAL(k,j) where max(m-n,k-j) + max(j,n) <= 18	DECIMAL(18, max(j,n))
	DECIMAL(k,j) where max(m-n,k-j) + max(j,n) > 18	DECIMAL (38, max(j,n))
BYTEINT SMALLINT INTEGER BIGINT DECIMAL(m,n) NUMBER(m,n) NUMBER(m) NUMBER(*,n) NUMBER	NUMBER(k,j) NUMBER(k) NUMBER(*,j) NUMBER	NUMBER
DATE	BYTEINT SMALLINT INTEGER	INTEGER
	BIGINT	BIGINT
	FLOAT	FLOAT
FLOAT	BYTEINT SMALLINT INTEGER	FLOAT

	BIGINT DECIMAL(m,n) NUMBER(m,n) NUMBER(m) NUMBER(*,n) NUMBER	

Period	Character	Period
TIMESTAMP	DATE	DATE
TIMESTAMP WITH TIME ZONE		
Interval The INTERVAL type must have only one field, e.g. INTERVAL YEAR	Exact Numeric	Numeric

Figure 11.2

The following table identifies data types on which Teradata Database does not perform implicit type conversions.

Type	**Rules**
BYTE	Byte data types can only be compared with byte data types. Attempts to compare a byte type with another type produce an error.
TIME	Teradata Database does not perform implicit type conversion from TIME to TIMESTAMP and from TIMESTAMP to TIME in comparison operations.
TIMESTAMP	
UDT	Teradata Database does not perform implicit type conversion on UDTs for comparison operations. A UDT value can only be compared with another value of the same UDT type.

	To compare UDTs with other data types, you must use explicit data type conversion.

Figure 11.3

Implicit numeric to character conversions can result in truncation, as shown in the next figure.

```
CT loss(c1 INT, c2 CHAR(4));
INS loss VALUES(1, '1234');
INS loss VALUES(2, 2345);
SEL * FROM loss ORDER BY 1;

         c1  c2
-----------  ----
          1  1234
          2    23
```

Figure 11.4

Store numbers in numeric data types, or use CAST. Remember, storage and display are two separate issues.

Full Table Scans

Though full table scans harness the parallel processing of the Teradata Database, they should be minimized to allow a greater workflow.

Full table scans can be caused by:

- The lack of a WHERE clause.
- A WHERE clause that doesn't reference any index.
- Inequality index access.
- A WHERE clause that supplies a numeric value for a character index and causes implicit data conversion.

- Stale statistics.
- No statistics.
- Weakly-selective NUSIs.
- NoPI tables lacking any Secondary or Join Indexes.
- Not supplying a value for all columns of a composite index.
- No static partition elimination possible.
- No delayed row partition elimination possible.

Use the EXPLAIN facility to analyze your WHERE clause statements for opportunities to eliminate full table scans.

Aggregations

Aggregation is a two-step process.

1. Each AMP aggregates its own rows locally as the parallel first step in the global parallel aggregation process.
2. Then the fields in the GROUP BY key are hashed, and the resulting hash bucket for each distinct value points to the AMP responsible for building the global aggregate for that piece of the aggregation.

If you have a large table that is aggregated frequently, consider either creating an AGI, or creating and maintaining your own summary table.

Partitioned Primary Indexes are designed to optimize range-based queries while providing efficient Primary Index join strategies. There are tradeoffs between improving range access and doing aggregations on the primary index as well as PI access and joins, which is a function of the number of populated row partitions that exist.

Though the system supports the nesting of views, avoid any nesting of aggregate views. If an aggregate view references another aggregate view, the aggregation in both views will have to be done individually, adding to the system overhead. The next example shows this.

```
CV v1 AS SEL dept_no, SUM(salary) AS sum_sal
FROM employee_table GROUP BY dept_no;
CV v2 AS SEL SUM(sum_sal) AS tot_sal FROM v1;
EXPLAIN SEL * FROM v2;
```

```
Explanation
-----------------------------------------------------------
  1) First, we lock a distinct CSQL_CLASS."pseudo table"
for read on a RowHash to prevent global deadlock for
CSQL_CLASS.employee_table.
  2) Next, we lock CSQL_CLASS.employee_table in view v2 for
read.
  3) We do an all-AMPs SUM step to aggregate from
CSQL_CLASS.employee_table in view v2 by way of an all-rows
scan with no residual conditions , grouping by field1
(CSQL_CLASS.employee_table.Dept_No. Aggregate Intermediate
Results are computed globally, then placed in Spool 3. The
size of Spool 3 is estimated with high confidence to be 6
rows (138 bytes).  The estimated time for this step is 0.05
seconds.
  4) We do an all-AMPs RETRIEVE step from Spool 3 (Last
Use) by way of an all-rows scan into Spool 1 (used to
materialize view, derived table or table function v1)
(all_amps), which is built locally on the AMPs. The size of
Spool 1 is estimated with high confidence to be 6 rows (174
bytes). The estimated time for this step is 0.04 seconds.
  5) We do an all-AMPs SUM step to aggregate from Spool 1
(Last Use) by way of an all-rows scan.  Aggregate
Intermediate Results are computed globally, then placed in
Spool 7.  The size of Spool 7 is estimated with high
confidence to be 1 row (23 bytes).  The estimated time for
this step is 0.06 seconds.
  6) We do an all-AMPs RETRIEVE step from Spool 7 (Last
Use) by way of an all-rows scan into Spool 5 (group_amps),
which is built locally on the AMPs.  The size of Spool 5 is
estimated with high confidence to be 1 row (31 bytes).  The
estimated time for this step is 0.02 seconds.
  7) Finally, we send out an END TRANSACTION step to all
AMPs involved in processing the request.
  -> The contents of Spool 5 are sent back to the user as
the result of statement 1. The total estimated time is 0.17
seconds.
```

Figure 11.5

Nested Views

Explaining a request does not necessarily report the names of all the underlying database objects accessed by that request, but it does provide the names of all the base tables accessed.

If you need to determine all the objects a particular view accesses, including any nested views, use the SHOW QUALIFIED statement For example, the following request reports the create text and containing databases for all underlying tables and views accessed by *v2*.

SHOW QUALIFIED SELECT * FROM v2;

```
 *** Text of DDL statement returned.
 *** Total elapsed time was 1 second.
---------------------------------------------------------------------------
CREATE SET TABLE CSQL_CLASS.employee_table ,NO FALLBACK ,
     NO BEFORE JOURNAL,
     NO AFTER JOURNAL,
     CHECKSUM = DEFAULT,
     DEFAULT MERGEBLOCKRATIO
     (
      Employee_No INTEGER NOT NULL,
      Dept_No SMALLINT,
      Mgr_employee_no INTEGER,
      Last_name CHAR(20) CHARACTER SET LATIN NOT
      CASESPECIFIC,
      First_name VARCHAR(12) CHARACTER SET LATIN NOT
      CASESPECIFIC,
      Salary DECIMAL(8,2))
UNIQUE PRIMARY INDEX ( Employee_No )
INDEX ( Last_name )
INDEX ( Dept_No );

 *** Text of DDL statement returned.
---------------------------------------------------------------------------
CREATE VIEW "CSQL_CLASS"."v1" AS SELECT
"CSQL_CLASS"."employee_table"."Dept_No"
,SUM("CSQL_CLASS"."employee_table"."Salary" )(NAMED
"sum_sal" ) FROM "CSQL_CLASS"."employee_table"
GROUP BY "CSQL_CLASS"."employee_table"."Dept_No" ;

 *** Text of DDL statement returned.
---------------------------------------------------------------------------
CREATE VIEW "CSQL_CLASS"."v2" AS SELECT
SUM("CSQL_CLASS"."v1"."sum_sal" )(NAMED "tot_sal" ) FROM
"CSQL_CLASS"."v1" ;
```

Figure 11.6

Chapter 11: Practice Questions

1. To which of the join indexes below does the following SHOW JOIN INDEX output belong?

```
CREATE JOIN INDEX CSQL_CLASS.?????? ,NO FALLBACK
,CHECKSUM = DEFAULT AS
SELECT COUNT(*)(FLOAT, NAMED CountStar )
,CSQL_CLASS.employee_table.Dept_No
,SUM(CSQL_CLASS.employee_table.Salary )(DECIMAL(38,2),
NAMED tot_sal )
FROM CSQL_CLASS.employee_table
GROUP BY CSQL_CLASS.employee_table.Dept_No
PRIMARY INDEX ( Dept_No );
```

   a. CREATE JOIN INDEX indx_1 AS
      SELECT employee_no, dept_no, mgr_employee_no, last_name,first_name, salary
      FROM employee_table
      PRIMARY INDEX (mgr_employee_no);
   b. CREATE JOIN INDEX indx_2 AS
      SELECT employee_no, last_name, first_name, e.dept_no, department_name
      FROM employee_table AS e JOIN department_table AS d
      ON e.dept_no = d.dept_no;
   c. CREATE JOIN INDEX indx_3 AS
      SELECT count (*) (Named CountStar), d.dept_no, department_name, budget, SUM(salary) AS tot_sal
      FROM department_table AS d
      JOIN employee_table AS e
      ON d.dept_no = e.dept_no
      GROUP BY 2,3,4;

d. CREATE JOIN INDEX indx_4 AS
   SELECT *
   FROM employee_table
   PRIMARY INDEX (dept_no);
e. CREATE JOIN INDEX indx_5 AS
   SELECT COUNT(*)(FLOAT, NAMED CountStar), dept_no, SUM(salary) as tot_sal
   FROM employee_table
   GROUP BY 1;

2. What is the default flush rate for DBQL to write its internal buffers to disk?
   a. 2 minutes
   b. 5 minutes
   c. 8 minutes
   d. 10 minutes

3. Which of the following can have MERGEBLOCKRATIO applied? (Choose 2)
   a. Spool files
   b. Volatile tables
   c. Permanent journals
   d. Global temporary tables
   e. Permanent tables

4. What kind of table will be created by the following DDL statement?

   create table t1 as (select * from employee_table) with no data;

   a. NUPI MULTISET
   b. NUPI SET
   c. NUPI table kind default specified by the transaction mode
   d. UPI MULTISET
   e. UPI SET

5. Which of the following can be compared to other data types not listed?
   a. BYTE
   b. VARBYTE
   c. BLOB
   d. BYTEINT

Chapter Notes

Utilize this space for notes, key points to remember, diagrams, areas of further study, etc.

Chapter 12: Locks and Transactions

Certification Objectives

- ✓ Given a scenario, identify the effects of transaction isolation on locking.
- ✓ Given scenarios, determine appropriate situations where ANSI or Teradata mode should be used.
- ✓ Given a scenario, identify the effects of a system restart on utility locks.
- ✓ Given a scenario, identify the conflicting locks in a multi-statement request.
- ✓ Identify the performance considerations of lock acquisition.

Before You Begin

You should be familiar with the following terms and concepts.

Terms	Key Concepts
Locking Levels	Differences in Lock Levels
Utility Locks	ETL and ARC locks
ANSI Versus Teradata	Identify the differences
Merge-Into	How locks are deployed with the process

Any number of users and applications can simultaneously access data stored in a Teradata Database.

The Teradata Database Lock Manager imposes concurrency control by locking the database object being accessed by each transaction and releasing those locks when the transaction either commits or rolls back its work. This control ensures that the data remains consistent for all users. Note that with the exception of pseudo-table locks, locks in the Teradata Database are not managed globally, but by each AMP individually.

Teradata locks and Levels

Teradata can apply locks at the database level, the table level, or at the row level. It does this by locking the 32-bit Database ID, the 32-bit Table ID, or a 32-bit Row Hash.

A lock applied to a database id, automatically locks all objects in that database. A lock applied to a table id, locks up all of the indexes and rows in that table. A lock applied to a row hash, locks up all of the rows in a table having that value.

Remember, every row in the entire system is uniquely identified by the following 32-bit system values.

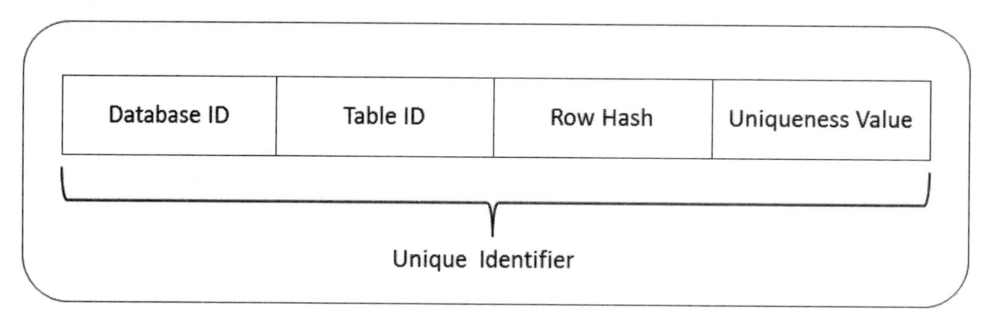

Figure 12.1

Locking levels determine the type of object that is locked and the impact on other users, as follows:

LOCKING LEVEL	**Resource(s) unavailable to other users**
DATABASE	All tables, views, macros and triggers owned by the database/user
VIEW	All tables referenced in the View
TABLE	All rows in the base table and in any secondary index and fallback subtables associated with it
ROW	The primary copy of rows sharing the same row hash value A row hash lock permits other users to access other data in the table and is the least restrictive type of automatic lock A row hash lock applies to a *set* of rows that shares the same hash code. It does not necessarily, nor even generally, lock only one row • A row hash lock is applied whenever a table is accessed using a *primary index (PI)* • For an update that uses a *unique secondary index (USI)*, the appropriate row of the secondary index subtable is also locked • It is not necessary to lock the fallback copy of the row, nor any associated row, of a *nonunique secondary index* (NUSI) subtable

Figure 12.2

Locks Strategies and Compatibility

The types of locks and their descriptions are:

LOCK TYPE	DESCRIPTION
ACCESS	• Permits selection of data from a base table that can be locked for write by other users • Placing an ACCESS lock requires the SELECT privilege on the specified object
READ	• Ensures data consistency during a read operation such as a SELECT request • This is the default lock on SELECT statements • Multiple users can concurrently hold a READ lock on a base table. As long as a READ lock is in place, no modification of the object is allowed • Placing a READ lock requires the SELECT privilege on the specified object • SHARE is a synonym for READ
WRITE	• Enables a single user to modify data • This is the default for INSERT, UPDATE, and DELETE statements • As long as the WRITE lock is in place, all other users are excluded from viewing or modifying the object except readers who are viewing data using an ACCESS lock • Until a WRITE lock is released, no new READ locks are permitted on the locked object • Placing a WRITE lock requires an UPDATE, INSERT, or DELETE privilege on the specified object
EXCLUSIVE	• Excludes all other users • This is the most restrictive lock • EXCLUSIVE locks are rarely used except to make structural changes to a database

LOCK TYPE	DESCRIPTION
	• This is the default on all DDL statements • Placing an EXCLUSIVE lock on a database object requires the DROP privilege on that object
CHECKSUM	• Used only with updatable cursors in embedded SQL and stored procedures

Figure 12.3

When a lock is requested, the system will either Grant the lock, or put the request into the lock Queue as follows:

	LOCK REQUESTED			
LOCK HELD	**ACCESS**	**READ**	**WRITE**	**EXCLUSIVE**
None	Grant	Grant	Grant	Grant
ACCESS	Grant	Grant	Grant	**Queue**
READ	Grant	Grant	**Queue**	**Queue**
WRITE	Grant	**Queue**	**Queue**	**Queue**
EXCLUSIVE	**Queue**	**Queue**	**Queue**	**Queue**

Figure 12.4

Any lock can be upgraded, but only a READ lock can be downgraded to an ACCESS lock.

Locking Modifiers

Use the LOCKING modifier to change a lock. Here are the syntax formats of the LOCKING Modifier:

```
LOCKING [<table-name>] FOR <desired-locking> [NOWAIT]
LOCKING ROW FOR <desired-locking> [NOWAIT]
LOCKING DATABASE <database-name> FOR <desired-locking>
[NOWAIT]
LOCKING VIEW <view-name> FOR <desired-locking> [NOWAIT]
LOCKING TABLE <table-name> FOR <desired-locking> [NOWAIT]
```

Figure 12.5

The NOWAIT Option

NOWAIT instructs the system to abort the request if the lock cannot be granted immediately. Without this option, a request will wait indefinitely for a locked resource. Specify this option for situations in which it is not desirable to have a request wait for resources, and possibly tie up resources another request could be using.

Utility Locks

FASTLOAD and TPT LOAD

A paused Teradata FastLoad job is one that was halted during the loading or end loading phase before completing. The paused condition can be intentional, or the result of an error condition or a system failure.

When a FastLoad job is in the paused state, the target table and the two error tables are locked.

ARCHIVE and RECOVERY (ARC)

A Host Utility (HUT) lock is the lock that Teradata ARC places when most Teradata ARC commands are executed. Exceptions are **CHECKPOINT**, **DELETE DATABASE**, and **DELETE JOURNAL**. When Teradata ARC places a HUT lock on an object, the following conditions apply:

- HUT locks are associated with the currently logged-on user who entered the statement, not with a job or transaction.
- HUT locks are placed only on the AMPs that are participating in a Teradata ARC operation.
- A HUT lock that is placed for a user on an object at one level *never* conflicts with another level of lock on the same object for the same user.

MULTILOAD and TPT UPDATE

MultiLoad uses two kinds of long-term locks on the tables involved in a MultiLoad task:

- Utilizes an Access lock to prevent DDL activities.
- Applies an Exclusive lock when it enters the Application Phase.

The locking levels are imposed by the utility for:

- MultiLoad import or delete tasks, including all MultiLoad utility commands except RELEASE MLOAD
- End phase target table rebuilds in AMPs marked as down for MultiLoad tasks
- Rebuild logic triggered by target table I/O errors

The most restrictive exclusive lock is used only when a RELEASE MLOAD statement is executed after a MultiLoad task has been suspended or aborted.

Showlocks

The Show Locks utility, *showlocks*, provides information about Host Utility (HUT) locks placed on databases and tables by the Archive/Recovery (ARC) utility during database operations.

Release Lock Commands

During an archive or recovery operation, the ARC utility places HUT locks on the objects affected by the operation, which remain active during a Teradata Database or client restart. These locks must be explicitly released by the RELEASE LOCK statement or by including the RELEASE LOCK keywords on the ARCHIVE, REVALIDATE REFERENCES FOR, ROLLBACK, ROLLFORWARD, RESTORE and BUILD statements. Teradata ARC issues a message to report when the release operation is complete. If any AMPs are offline, ARC releases HUT locks when the AMPs return to online operation.

ANSI Versus Teradata Mode

ANSI

In ANSI mode, transactions are always *explicit*. Each ANSI transaction is *implicitly* initiated, but always *explicitly* completed.

A transaction begins with the first request submitted in a session and continues until the system encounters either an explicit COMMIT statement or an explicit ROLLBACK statement, at which point it ends, releasing all the locks it held, discarding the Transient Journal, and closing any open cursors.

Teradata

Transactions can be implicit or explicit. Unless bounded by explicit BEGIN TRANSACTION (BT) and END TRANSACTION (ET) statements, the system treats each request as an implicit transaction.

Explicit transaction boundaries are specified using BEGIN TRANSACTION (BT) and END TRANSACTION (ET). BTET means that you can optionally code transaction initiation and termination explicitly in Teradata session mode, but not in ANSI session mode.

When a transaction fails, the system first rolls the transaction back automatically, discards its Transient Journal, releases all locks, and closes any open cursors. Statement Failure responses roll back the entire transaction, not just the request that evokes them.

Multi-Statement Serialization Locks

The definition of serializability is that any arbitrary execution of concurrent database access by transactions preserves the integrity of the database. This means that if transaction T1 and Transaction T2 are executing concurrently, it appears to each transaction that the other transaction executed either before or after it. This is accomplished through locking.

The level of locking (database, tab le, row hash), and the severity of the lock (exclusive, write, read, access) prevents other concurrently running transactions from making illegal interventions. Since the system only places locks at the database, table, or row hash level, individual partitions of an SLPPI or MLPPI table cannot be locked.

Teradata uses a two-phase locking protocol. This means that the system will not request additional locks for a transaction after it releases the locks it already has. Teradata acquires all of the locks for a transaction at the very beginning, and holds those locks until the transaction ends.

Locking only ensures the consistent state of the database, not some particular ordering of transaction execution.

Note: When using Macros, or statements within a Begin Transaction / End Transaction (BTET), you could conceivable create an unforeseen deadlock scenario from separate, concurrent requests. For example, one scenario is where a transaction(x) may wait for a lock held by another transaction (y) to be released and simultaneously, transaction(y) is waiting for a transaction(x) lock to be released (aka DEADLOCK).

Merge-Into Locks

The behavior of MERGE requests is affected based on the locking levels set by you or the system. The Parser can process a MERGE request taking either the Original MERGE path or the ANSI MERGE path.

IF the Parser takes this path ...	THEN the system places these locks . . .
Original MERGE implementation from Teradata Database .	• Row Hash-level WRITE locks on the target table • READ or ACCESS locks on the source table depending on the situation and whether you specify a LOCKING request modifier
ANSI MERGE implementation from Teradata Database 14.0.	• Table-level WRITE locks on the target table • READ or ACCESS locks on the source table depending on the situation and whether you

IF the Parser takes this path . . .	THEN the system places these locks . . .
	specify a LOCKING request modifier

Figure 12.6

Note: These considerations must be clearly understood when you write your MERGE requests.

Chapter 12: Practice Questions

1. Which of the following is not a Teradata lock?
    a. ACCESS
    b. EXCLUSIVE
    c. NOWAIT
    d. READ
    e. WRITE

2. What locks will be applied to:

    LOCKING ROW FOR WRITE SELECT * FROM job_table;

    a. ACCESS
    b. READ
    c. WRITE
    d. EXCLUSIVE

3. What lock does MultiLoad use in the Application Phase?
    a. ACCESS
    b. READ
    c. WRITE
    d. EXCLUSIVE

4. Which command is used to remove HUT locks after a client or Teradata Database restart?
    a. RELEASE LOCK
    b. CANCEL LOCK
    c. REMOVE LOCK
    d. KILL LOCK

5. At what level can locks be placed on PPI tables? (Choose 2)
    a. Entire table
    b. Individual partitions (SLPPI only)
    c. An individual partition and its sub-partitions (MLPPI)
    d. Row Hash
    e. An individual sub-partition

Chapter Notes

Utilize this space for notes, key points to remember, diagrams, areas of further study, etc.

Chapter 13: Databases, Objects, Manipulations, and Management

Certification Objectives

- ✓ Describe the performance characteristics of UNICODE character sets.
- ✓ Describe the performance considerations of Referential Integrity.
- ✓ Given a scenario about designing a database hierarchy, identify the characteristics of databases and users.
- ✓ Given a scenario, describe the use of a Queue Table.
- ✓ Given a scenario, determine the performance impact of using a SET or MULTISET table.
- ✓ Given a scenario, identify which data types are appropriate.

Before You Begin

You should be familiar with the following terms and concepts.

Terms	Key Concepts
Data Types	What is supported by Teradata and best practices
Databases and Users	Primary differences and characteristics
Table Options	Considerations for and implementation options
Merge Into	How to utilize and compare to other methods

Databases and Users

Users and databases are the logical repositories that make up a Teradata Database system. Users and databases contain other database objects such as tables, views, and macros. Databases and users may own, and be owned by, other databases and users in a hierarchy.

The primary difference between a database and a user is that you cannot log on as a database.

By default, when you first install Teradata Database on your server, it creates a user called DBC. This user owns the majority of the databases and users in the system.

Database Space Considerations

User DBC also initially owns all the space in the entire system. As you create new databases and users, you subtract available permanent space from User DBC. A database or user that has space subtracted from its own permanent space to create a new object becomes the immediate owner of that new object. User DBC is the owner of all subsequent owners in the entire database.

The following figure is an example of creating a hierarchy of databases and users:

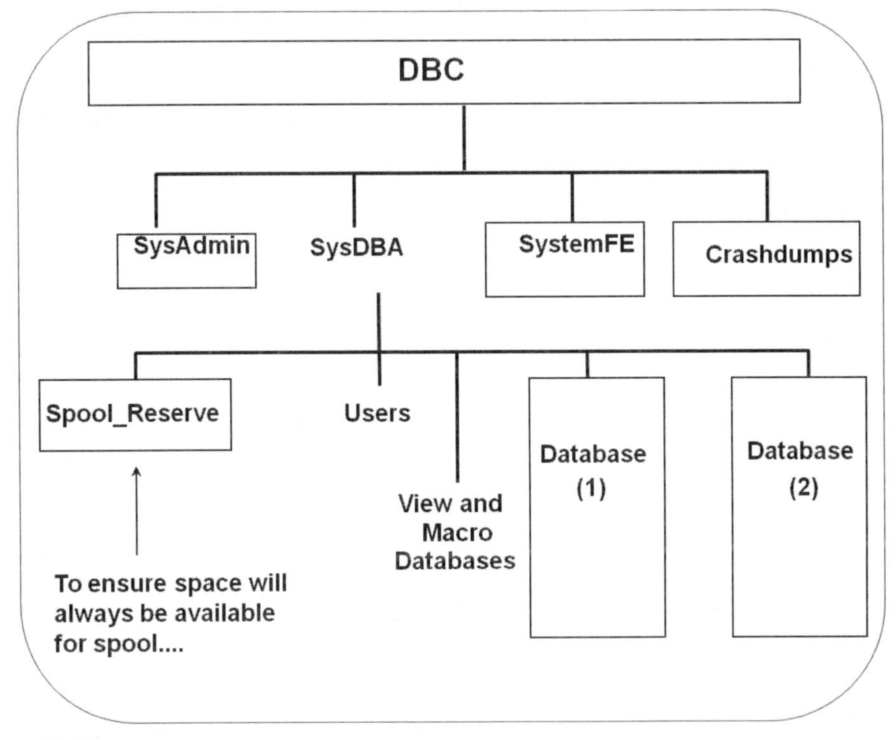

Figure 13.1

Data Types

All data in a database will have characteristics associated with it called attributes. Attributes would include a data type and length.

- A data type specifies the type and format of the data.
- The data value must conform to the rules and characteristics of the data type.
- A column in a relational database may only store one type of data and data types may not be mixed.
- Teradata supports most standard ANSI data types.

Teradata allows you to use either the specific data type name, or the data type alias, when defining a column's data type, but will actually use the full data type name on the table definition.

Note: SQL will convert data types when necessary. However, unintended data type conversions may not perform optimally. Domains for columns that will be joined together should be of the same data type or data type family for best results.

Byte

Data Type	ANSI SQL	Teradata Extension
BLOB[(n)]	X	
BYTE[(n)]		X
VARBYTE[(n)]		X

Numeric

Data Type	ANSI SQL	Teradata Extension
BIGINT	X	
BYTEINT		X
DATE[a]		X
DECIMAL[(n[,m])]	X	
DOUBLE PRECISION	X	
FLOAT [n]	X	
INTEGER	X	
NUMERIC[(n[,m])]	X	
REAL	X	
SMALLINT	X	

DateTime

Data Type	ANSI SQL	Teradata Extension
DATE[a]	X	
TIME [(n)]	X	

Data Type	ANSI SQL	Teradata Extension
TIME [(n)] WITH TIME ZONE	X	
TIMESTAMP [(n)]	X	
TIMESTAMP [(n)] WITH TIME ZONE	X	

Interval

Data Type	ANSI SQL	Teradata Extension
INTERVAL	X	
INTERVAL DAY[(n)] TO HOUR	X	
INTERVAL DAY [(n)] TO MINUTE	X	
INTERVAL DAY [(n)] TO SECOND	X	
INTERVAL HOUR[(n)]	X	
INTERVAL HOUR [(n)] TO MINUTE	X	
INTERVAL HOUR [(n)] TO SECOND	X	
INTERVAL MINUTE [(n)]	X	
INTERVAL MINUTE [(n)] TO SECOND [(m)]	X	
INTERVAL MONTH [(n)]	X	
INTERVAL SECOND [n[,m])]	X	
INTERVAL YEAR	X	
INTERVAL YEAR TO [(n)] TO MONTH	X	

Character

Data Type	ANSI SQL	Teradata Extension
CHAR [(n)]	X	
CLOB	X	
CHAR VARYING (n)	X	
LONG VARCHAR		X
VARCHAR (n)	X	

Graphic[b]

Data Type	ANSI SQL	Teradata Extension
GRAPHIC [(n)]		X
LONG VARGRAPHIC		X
VARGRAPHIC (n)		X

UDT

Data Type	ANSI SQL	Teradata Extension
udt_name[c]	X	

Figure 13.2

Notes:

- **DATE**[a] is supported both in its Teradata and ANSI DateTime form.
- **GRAPHIC**[b] types are equivalent to the type CHARACTER SET GRAPHIC, which is the form to use for all new development.
- The CREATE TYPE statement determines the name of a **UDT**[c].

Byte Data	**Description**
BLOB	Binary Large Object Max: 2,097,088,000 bytes which is the default
BYTE (size)	Fixed length Binary string Default: (1) Max: 64,000 bytes
VARBYTE (size)	Variable length Binary string Default: (1) Max: 64,000 bytes

Numeric Data	**Description**
BIGINT	Whole number

<table>
<tr><th>Numeric Data</th><th>Description</th></tr>
<tr><td></td><td>Range: -9,233,372,036,854,775,807 to 9,233,372,036,854,775,807
8 bytes with the least significant byte first</td></tr>
<tr><td>BYTEINT</td><td>Whole number
Range: -128 to 127
1 byte</td></tr>
<tr><td>SMALLINT</td><td>Whole number
Range: -32,768 to 32,767
2 bytes</td></tr>
<tr><td>INTEGER</td><td>Whole number
Range: -2,147,483,648 to 2,147,483,647
4 bytes</td></tr>
<tr><td>DECIMAL [(n[,m])]</td><td>Decimal number of n digits, with m digits to the right of the decimal point
Default: DECIMAL(5,0)
<table>
<tr><td>Number of digits (n)</td><td>Number of bytes</td></tr>
<tr><td>1 to 2</td><td>1</td></tr>
<tr><td>3 to 4</td><td>2</td></tr>
<tr><td>5 to 9</td><td>4</td></tr>
<tr><td>10 to 18</td><td>8</td></tr>
<tr><td>19 to 38</td><td>16</td></tr>
</table></td></tr>
<tr><td>NUMERIC [(n [, m])]</td><td>Synonym for DECIMAL</td></tr>
<tr><td>FLOAT (n)</td><td>Floating Point number
IEEE format
Range: $2.226*10^{-308}$ to $1.797*10^{307}$
8 bytes</td></tr>
<tr><td>DOUBLE PRECISION</td><td>Synonym for FLOAT</td></tr>
<tr><td>REAL</td><td>Synonym for FLOAT</td></tr>
</table>

Date/Time	Description
DATE	Special type of integer ((Calendar year) – 1900) + MM + DD Use ANSI Date form for compatibility 4 bytes

Date/Time	Description
TIME (n)	Stored as HHMMSS.nnnnnn 6 bytes
TIMESTAMP (n)	Stored as YYMMDDHHMMSS.nnnnnn 10 bytes
TIME (n) WITH TIME ZONE	Stored as HHMMSS.nnnnnn+HHMM 8 bytes
TIMESTAMP (n) WITH TIME ZONE	Stored as YYMMDDHHMMSS.nnnnnn+HHMM 12 bytes

Interval data types	Description
INTERVAL YEAR [(n)]	Number of years (n) = 1 to 4 digits for years Default = 2 2 bytes
INTERVAL MONTH [(n)]	Number of months (n) = 1 to 4 digits for months Default = 2 2 bytes
INTERVAL DAY [(n)]	Number of days (n) = 1 to 4 digits for days Default = 2 2 bytes
INTERVAL YEAR [(n)] TO MONTH	Number of years and months (n) = 1 to 4 digits for years Default = 2 4 bytes
INTERVAL HOUR [(n)]	Number of hours (n) = 1 to 4 digits for years Default = 2 2 bytes
INTERVAL MINUTE [(n)]	Number of minutes (n) = 1 to 4 digits for days Default = 2 2 bytes

Interval data types	Description
INTERVAL SECOND [(n)]	Number of seconds (n) = 1 to 4 digits for days Default = 2 (m) = 1 to 6 digits for fractional seconds Default = 6 6 bytes
INTERVAL DAY [(n)] TO HOUR	Number of days and hours (n) = 1 to 4 digits for days Default = 2 4 bytes
INTERVAL DAY [(n)] TO MINUTE	Number of days, hours and minutes (n) = 1 to 4 digits for days Default = 2 HOUR is always 2 digits and MINUTE is always 2 digits 8 bytes
INTERVAL DAY [(n)] TO SECOND [(m)]	Number of days, hours, minutes, and seconds (n) = 1 to 4 digits for days Default = 2 (m) = 1 to 6 digits for fractional seconds Default = 6 10 bytes
INTERVAL HOUR TO MINUTE	Number of hours and minutes (n) = 1 to 4 digits for hours Default = 2 4 bytes
INTERVAL HOUR [(n)] TO SECOND [(m)]	Number of hours, minutes and seconds (n) = 1 to 4 digits for hours Default = 2 (m) = 1 to 6 digits for fractional seconds Default = 6 8 bytes
INTERVAL MINUTE [(n)] TO SECOND	Number of minutes and seconds (n) = 1 to 4 digits for minutes

Interval data types	Description
[(m)]	Default = 2 (m) = 1 to 6 digits for fractional seconds Default = 6 6 bytes

Character / Graphic Data Types	Description
CHAR (size)	Fixed length character data Max: 64,000
CLOB	Character Large Object Max: 2,097,088,000 which is the default
VARCHAR (size) or CHARACTER VARYING (size)	Variable length character data Max: 64,000
LONG VARCHAR	Equivalent to VARCHAR(64000)
GRAPHIC (size)	Fixed length graphic data 2 bytes per character Max: 32,000 double-byte characters
LONG VARGRAPHIC	Fixed length graphic data 32,000 double-byte characters
VARGRAPHIC (size)	Variable length graphic data 2 bytes per character Max: 32,000 double-byte characters

Figure 13.3

CREATE TABLE Attributes

Besides defining the columns and indexes, the CREATE TABLE statement has the following attributes. All of the attributes have defaults.

```
CREATE [SET/MULTISET] [VOLATILE/GLOBAL TEMPORARY]
TABLE tablename
        <Create Table Options>
        <Column Definitions>
        <Table-level Constraints>
        <Index Definitions>;
```

Figure 13.4

Where:

Create Table options	Specify physical attributes of table: Fallback Journaling Freespace Datablocksize
Column definitions	Define each column's data type, attributes, and any constraints: ○ PRIMARY KEY ○ UNIQUE ○ CHECK ○ REFERENCES
Table-level constraints	Define multi-column constraints: PRIMARY KEY FOREIGN KEY UNIQUE CHECK conditions
Index definitions	Specify indexes for physical access to data

Row retention	COMMIT options

Figure 13.5

CREATE TABLE AS Attributes

Use the CREATE TABLE AS command to create a new table from the results of a query. Syntax for the CREATE TABLE AS is:

```
CREATE [ VOLATILE | GLOBAL TEMPORARY ] TABLE <tablename>
[ (<column_name> [, ...] ) ]
AS <select_clause> [ Primary Index (<column-list>) ]
WITH [ NO ] DATA;
```

Figure 13.6

The example below illustrates a CREATE TABLE AS function:

```
CREATE TABLE order_table_new AS (SELECT * from order_table)
WITH DATA ;
```

Figure 13.7

You can only create the structure for a global temporary table, but not its data.

Duplicate Row Option

- SET
- MULITSET

Table type options:

- Permanent – This is the default.

- VOLATILE – exists only for the duration of the user's session.
- GLOBAL TEMPORARY– definition is permanent, but data exists only for the duration of the user's session.

Table protection options:

- [NO] FALLBACK PROTECTION
- [NO] LOG
- [NO|DUAL] BEFORE JOURNAL
- [NO|DUAL|LOCAL|[NOT] LOCAL] AFTER JOURNAL
- FREESPACE = n [PERCENT] (percentage of cylinder freespace)
- DATABLOCKSIZE = n BYTES (maximum data block size)

SET Versus MULTISET

As shown above, this attribute defines duplicate row control. A SET table cannot have duplicate rows. A MULTISET may have duplicate rows. If there are uniqueness constraints on any column or set of columns in the table definition, then the table cannot have duplicate rows even if it is declared as MULTISET. The default in ANSI mode is MULTISET. The default in Teradata mode is SET.

Queue Tables

A queue table is a special persistent table used to handle queue-oriented data. Examples are asynchronous data loading applications with subsequent complex processing of the buffered data load and event processing. The properties of queue tables are similar to those of ordinary base tables, with the additional unique property of behaving like an asynchronous first-in-first-out (FIFO) queue.

You can think of a queue table as a regular table that also has a memory-resident cache associated with it that tracks the FIFO queue ordering of its rows. Consumed rows are retrieved and deleted from the database simultaneously, which ensures that no row can be processed more than once.

Because most, if not all, rows for a given queue table are memory-resident on a PE, they are processed similarly to primary index operations made against non-queue tables, which are single-AMP operations applied with a Row Hash WRITE lock on the row.

Row ordering in a queue table is not guaranteed to be truly FIFO for the following reasons:

- The system clocks on MPP system nodes are not synchronized.
- The QITS value for a row might be user-supplied or updated, either of which could change its position in the queue.
- A transaction rollback restores rows with their original QITS value, which might be an earlier value than rows that have already been consumed.
- Insert operations within the same multi-statement request might be assigned the same QITS value.
- If Teradata Workload Manager is enabled, one or more rules might defer consume mode operations from running. As a general rule, do not create rules that affect SELECT AND CONSUME operations because such workload restrictions can easily lead to queue table rows being processed in an order that differs significantly from a "true" FIFO.
- It is also true that the query scheduler might never see a queue table row because a consume mode operation might delete the row before it qualifies for a query scheduler rule.

An ideal queue table has the following characteristics:

- Low cardinality (implying that its rows are consumed at roughly the same rate as they are inserted).
- Infrequent UPDATE operations to its rows.
- Infrequent DELETE operations on its rows.

A queue table might be used to process event alerts.

- When an incident is detected by an application, it can insert data from that incident into an event queue table by means of a trigger.
- An external event-processing application could then extract events from the queue table by submitting a SELECT AND CONSUME TOP 1 statement. The SELECT AND CONSUME TOP 1 waits for data to be inserted into the queue table.
- When data arrives at the queue, the waiting SELECT AND CONSUME TOP 1 statement returns the result to the external application, which then processes the data further.
- The external application might then loop and submit another SELECT AND CONSUME TOP 1 statement to wait for further event data to be inserted into the queue table.
- This eliminates the need for polling loops which must blindly and repeatedly submit SELECT statements on non-queue tables, while waiting for an event to occur.

SYNTAX

```
CREATE [SET/MULTISET] TABLE tablename, QUEUE [ , <Create Table Options> ]
        ( QITS_column_name TIMESTAMP(6) NOT NULL
            DEFAULT CURRENT_TIMESTAMP(6)
            [ <data_attributes> <constraints> ]
        [ , <Additional Column Definitions> ] )
        <Table-level Constraints>
        <Index Definitions>;
```

Figure 13.8

The first column defined for any queue table must be a Query Insertion Timestamp (QITS) column. The system uses the QITS column to maintain the FIFO ordering of rows in the queue table.

Each queue table has only one QITS column, and it must be defined with the following attributes:

- *column_name* TIMESTAMP(6) NOT NULL DEFAULT CURRENT_TIMESTAMP(6)

The precision specification is optional for the TIMESTAMP data type specification and its DEFAULT attribute, but you cannot define either with a precision value other than 6.

The QITS column *cannot* be defined as any of the following:

- UNIQUE PRIMARY INDEX
- UNIQUE
- PRIMARY KEY
- Unique secondary index
- Identity column

The QITS column can be the NUPI for a table, but you should avoid following that practice.

Keep in mind that if you do not define an explicit primary index, primary key, or uniquely constrained column in the table, then the QITS column becomes its primary index by default because it is the first column defined for the table.

You might find it useful to define additional queue management columns for such things as message identification or queue sequencing.

Tables - Rename, Alter, Drop

To change the name of a database object, use the RENAME command. The general syntax is:

```
RENAME { TABLE | VIEW | MACRO } [ databasename. ] oldobjectname
{ TO | AS }
[ databasename. ] newobjectname ;
```

Figure 13.9

Through the ALTER TABLE [*databasename.*] *tablename* command, you can:

ADD/MODIFY	FALLBACK
ADD/MODIFY	BEFORE/AFTER journaling
ADD/MODIFY	CHECKSUM
ADD/MODIFY	FREESPACE
ADD/MODIFY	DATABLOCKSIZE
ADD/DROP/RENAME	Columns
ADD/DROP	FOREIGN KEY constraints
DROP	INCONSISTENT REFERENCES
ADD/DROP/MODIFY	CHECK constraints
DROP	Constraints
ADD	UNIQUE constraints
ADD	PRIMARY KEY constraints
MODIFY	Partitioned Primary Indexes
REVALIDATE	Partitioned Primary Indexes

Figure 13.10

To remove a table, view, or macro from a database, use the DROP command. The general syntax is:

DROP { TABLE | VIEW | MACRO } [*databasename.*] *objectname* ;

Figure 13.11

There are times when it's appropriate to create a new table rather than altering a table. Keep in mind that an ALTER table requires an EXCLUSIVE lock and cannot be accessed while the operation is performed. If consumers require high data availability then perhaps an alternative approach, such as creating a new table built with rows from the current table, may be a better option.

An example is a large production table that is heavily utilized and maintenance is required (i.e. changing columns / deleting large amounts of data). In this case, the best practice would be to create a new table with the changes, insert/ select data to new, collect stats on new, rename old to new2, and then rename new to old when ready for the change. Then drop new2.

Column Attributes

COLUMN ATTRIBUTE	DEFINITION
UPPERCASE | UC	Store character data in UPPERCASE automatically The default is mixed case
[NOT] CASESPECIFIC	Teradata mode = NOT CASESPECIFIC ANSI mode = CASESPECIFIC
FORMAT	Defines an edit mask for display
TITLE	Titles are for display only. They cannot be referenced within a query. TITLEs can be stacked up to three lines
NAMED	Change the column name for display and reference
DEFAULT	Define a value to be inserted into the

COLUMN ATTRIBUTE	DEFINITION
	column if one is not specified
WITH DEFAULT	Insert the system default value
CHARACTER SET LATIN UNICODE GRAPHIC KANJISJIS* KANJI*	The server character set for the character column being defined. *The use of KANJI is deprecated. Upon upgrading to Teradata Database 14.0 or greater, the system automatically replaces DEFAULT CHARACTER SET KANJI1 with DEFAULT CHARACTER SET UNICODE in existing user definitions.
[NOT] NULL	Whether null values will be allowed
COMPRESS	Whether occurrences of specific values should be compressed as a space-saving technique
UNIQUE	Disallow duplicate values. The column must also be declared NOT NULL. Will be enforced as a unique index
PRIMARY KEY	The column must also be declared NOT NULL. Will be enforced as a unique index
CHECK	A Boolean expression to be applied on INSERT and UPDATE

Figure 13.12

Unicode Data Types

The UNICODE server character set supports 16-bit characters from the Unicode 4.1 standard. When a system or user table is created for Japanese systems, the default is UNICODE.

Each code point represents a distinct character, including non-spacing characters such as diacritical marks and joiners. All characters named as letters in UNICODE are considered as such, and are candidates for uppercasing. Many code points in Unicode are either unassigned in Unicode 4.1 or reserved (for example surrogates). Such code points may not be stored as UNICODE character data. Database storage space for UNICODE is allocated on a character basis.

Note: When using UNICODE, you need to take into consideration the encode/decode processing which will have an impact on row inserts. Also, UNICODE doubles the storage requirement for each column that uses it.

Insert/Select Considerations

This command is used to copy rows, or a subset of rows, from one table to another. A simple INSERT/SELECT:

```
INSERT INTO emp_new
SELECT * FROM employee_table ;
```

Figure 13.13

Assumes:

1. emp_new and employee_table have the same definitions.
2. a complete replica of employee_table is required.

Two different optimizations can occur:

1. If the PI of the source AND destination tables are identical, an AMP local operation is used.
2. If the target table is empty,
    a. Transient Journaling is reduced
    b. 64K block transfers are used

If both conditions are satisfied, both optimizations are used.

Update/Insert Considerations

Teradata has another extension to the Update command called an upsert (UPDATE ... ELSE INSERT ...)

```
UPDATE job_table
SET job_desc = 'Gopher'
WHERE job_no = 12345  /* Non-existent job number */
ELSE
INSERT INTO job_table
VALUES (12345, 'Gopher');
```

Figure 13.14

Below are general rules you need to follow when doing an Upsert:

- You cannot perform atomic Upsert operations on tables with an identity column as their primary index.
- You can use the Upsert form of the UPDATE statement to order queue table rows.
- An Upsert can be triggering event, or triggering statement.

Merge Into Considerations

This command merges a source row set into a target table based on whether any target rows satisfy a specified matching condition with the source row. It acts like an upsert, but over more than one row. The target table can be a base data table, global temporary table, volatile table, or queue table to be updated, inserted into, or both.

The placement of the INSERT specification before or after the UPDATE specification will change the order of trigger firing.

Merge with matched updates and unmatched inserts steps assume that the source table is always distributed on the join column of the source table, which is specified in the ON clause as an equality constraint with the primary index of the target table and sorted on the RowKey. The step does a RowKey-based Merge Join internally, identifying source rows that qualify for updating target rows and source rows that qualify for inserts, after which it performs those updates and inserts. This step is very similar to the APPLY phase of MultiLoad because it guarantees that the target table data block is read and written only once during the MERGE operation.

Keep in mind the following when working with MERGE-INTO:

- The handling of duplicate rows on INSERT varies between ANSI mode and Teradata mode.

- The handling of duplicate rows on UPDATE varies depending on whether error logging is enabled.

- You cannot update primary index column values using MERGE.

- You cannot specify columns that reference tables other than the source or target tables for the MERGE request in the ON, WHEN MATCHED, or WHEN NOT MATCHED clauses.

The target table in a MERGE operation can have an identity column. The system generates numbers for MERGE inserts into the identity column in the same way it performs individual inserts into tables that do not have an identity column. Under most circumstances, the identity column cannot be the primary index for the target table.

If an insert or update to a row affects a partitioned table or partitioned join index, and the row partitioning expression doesn't result in a value between 1 and the number of partitions defined for that level, the system aborts the requests and returns an error.

Referential Integrity

Typically with relational databases, we need to ensure that a value that appears in one relation for a given set of attributes also appears for a certain set of attributes in another relation. This condition is called Referential integrity (RI). RI establishes relationships between tables, based on the definition of a primary key and a foreign key. The Teradata Database provides three choices to implement RI which are as follows:

- Use the referential constraint checks supplied by the database.
- Write site-specific macros.
- Enforce constraints through application code.

Teradata Database does provide a reliable mechanism to prevent accidental erasure or corruption of data in a database and ensuring data integrity and data consistency. The Referential Integrity Rules are outlined below.

- Every FK value set must match an existing PK value set
- The entire FK value set must be null

This is one of the fundamental principles of relational database theory, which is known as Hard Referential Integrity (Hard RI).

This above approach is typically used in OLTP transaction databases, but is not recommended for data warehousing. The best practice is to refrain from using Hard RI due to its high system resource cost and overhead. Data warehousing, in general, is optimized for READS not WRITES. In that regard, the alternate approach is to utilize Soft Referential Integrity (Soft RI). The benefit of SOFT RI (i.e. NO CHECK Option) is that Teradata provides for READ optimization because it can aid in 'dynamic join elimination' during a select transaction query execution saving system resources and runtime.

Following these rules ensures database integrity. Referential integrity constraints can also be used to optimize join plans in your physical data model.

Constraint Types

Teradata supports these column-level constraints:

UNIQUE	The column must be NOT NULL
PRIMARY KEY	The column must be NOT NULL
REFERENCES	A referential integrity reference to the parent table, not a view

Figure 13.15

The system also supports these multi-column table-level constraints:

UNIQUE	The columns must be NOT NULL
PRIMARY KEY	The columns must be NOT NULL
FOREIGN KEY	A referential integrity reference to the parent table, not a view

Figure 13.16

Notes:

- Constraints may be named (recommended) or unnamed.
- UDT, BLOB, or CLOB columns cannot be used to define a referential integrity relationship or other database constraint.
- You cannot specify REFERENCES constraints for identity columns, queue, global temporary, trace, or volatile tables.
- A REFERENCES constraint cannot reference a UDT or LOB column, nor columns in a queue table.

- When a CHECK constraint is part of the column definition, then its defined search condition cannot reference any other columns in its table, and set specifications are not allowed.

- You cannot define referential integrity constraints for a global temporary trace table.

Chapter 13: Practice Questions

1. Which of the following joins will perform the best?
    a. bigint JOIN float
    b. byte JOIN byteint
    c. smallint JOIN integer
    d. varchar JOIN vargraphic

2. Which numeric data type can hold the largest value?
    a. BIGINT
    b. DECIMAL
    c. INTEGER
    d. SMALLINT

3. Which Interval definition is invalid?
    a. YEAR TO MONTH
    b. MONTH TO DAY
    c. DAY TO HOUR
    d. DAY TO MINUTE
    e. DAY TO SECOND

4. CREATE TABLE . . . AS . . . WITH DATA; cannot be used to create which type of table?
    a. SET
    b. MULTISET
    c. VOLATILE
    d. GLOBAL TEMPORARY

5. To process rows from a queue table, an application should submit a ________ statement.
    a. CONSUME ALL
    b. READ AND CONSUME TOP 1
    c. SELECT AND CONSUME ALL
    d. SELECT AND CONSUME TOP 1

6. Which character set is deprecated and should not be used?
    a. Graphic
    b. Kanji
    c. Latin
    d. Unicode

Chapter Notes

Utilize this space for notes, key points to remember, diagrams, areas of further study, etc.

Chapter 14: Temporal Tables

Certification Objectives

- ✓ Given a scenario, design a SEQUENCED or NON-SEQUENCED temporal view.
- ✓ Given a scenario, design a temporal table.
- ✓ Given a scenario, design a temporal view using CURRENT time.
- ✓ Given a scenario, design an effective TRANSACTIONTIME table.
- ✓ Given a scenario, design an effective VALIDTIME table.
- ✓ Given a scenario, determine an effective method for implementing an AS OF view.

Before You Begin

You should be familiar with the following terms and concepts.

Terms	Key Concepts
PERIOD Data Types	How are they different than normal Temporal data types
VALIDTIME	What defines the boundaries for a row
TRANSACTIONTIME	What defines the boundaries for a row
Access Methods	SEQUENCED, NONSEQUENCED, AS OF, NONTEMPORAL, CURRENT

Period Temporal Data Types

A Period is an anchored duration of time. It has a beginning bound and an ending bound, and represents a set of contiguous time granules within that duration. The representation of the period extends from the beginning bound up to but not including the ending bound. In the following example, the period begins on January 1st, and ends on January 9th.

PERIOD(DATE '2011-01-01', DATE '2011-01-10')

Feature	Description
Temporal data types	The PERIOD data type represents an anchored duration of time.
Kinds of time	The elements of a PERIOD may be DATE, TIME, TIME WITH TIME ZONE, TIMESTAMP, or TIMESTAMP WITH TIME ZONE.
Temporal functions	These include BEGIN, END, LAST, INTERVAL, PRIOR, NEXT, P_INTERSECT, LDIFF, RDIFF, and P_NORMALIZE.

Figure 14.1

DateTime Granule

A DateTime granule is the minimum interval that can be represented at a given precision. As an example, if the element type of a period is DATE, the granule is one day. The last value of a period is the ending bound minus one granule of the element type.

Period Expressions

A Period definition takes the form:

PERIOD(<DateTime Expression> [, <DateTime Expression>])

If no ending bound is specified, then it is set to the beginning bound +1 granule, where the granule is derived from the data type.

A Period arithmetic expression takes the form:

<Period expression> +/- <Interval expression>
<Interval expression> +/- <Period expression>

A Period constant has the form of the PERIOD keyword followed by a quote string in a specific format. See the following examples.

Creating PERIOD Columns

The following is an example of creating and inserting a row into a period table.

```
CREATE TABLE period_table
(c1 INTEGER NOT NULL
,c2 PERIOD(DATE)
,c3 PERIOD(TIME(2))
,c4 PERIOD(TIME WITH TIME ZONE)
,c5 PERIOD(TIMESTAMP(4))
,c6 PERIOD(TIMESTAMP WITH TIME ZONE)
) PRIMARY INDEX(c1);
```

Figure 14.2

```
INSERT INTO period_table VALUES
(1
,PERIOD(DATE'2011-09-26', DATE'2011-10-01')
,PERIOD(TIME'11:22:33.44', TIME'11:33:33.44')
,PERIOD(TIME'09:09:09.000000+00:00',
TIME'10:10:10.000000+00:00')
,PERIOD(TIMESTAMP'2011-09-26 10:10:10.0000',
TIMESTAMP'2011-09-27 11:11:11.0000')
,PERIOD(TIMESTAMP'2011-09-26 12:34:56.123456+00:00',
TIMESTAMP'2011-09-27 01:01:01.654321+00:00')
);
```

Figure 14.3

The following query returns the row.

```
SET SESSION DATEFORM = ANSIDATE;
.SET FOLDLINE ON
.SET SIDETITLES ON
SELECT * FROM period_table;


 *** Query completed. One row found. 6 columns returned.
 *** Total elapsed time was 1 second.

c1           1
c2  ('11/09/26', '11/10/01')
c3  ('11:22:33.44', '11:33:33.44')
c4  ('09:09:09.000000+00:00', '10:10:10.000000+00:00')
c5  ('2011-09-26 10:10:10.0000', '2011-09-27 11:11:11.0000')
c6  ('2011-09-26 12:34:56.123456+00:00', '2011-09-27 01:01:01.654321+00:00')
```

Figure 14.4

UNTIL_CHANGED

UNTIL_CHANGED is used to represent the ending bound of periods for which the duration is indefinite or forever. It can also represent an unknown time in the future when the row will be changed. It is used, in some circumstances, when a new row is inserted into a temporal table:

The value of UNTIL_CHANGED depends on the data type and precision of the valid-time column.

1. If the type is PERIOD(DATE), UNTIL_CHANGED is the value DATE '9999-12-31'.

2. If the type is PERIOD(TIMESTAMP), UNTIL_CHANGED is the value of TIMESTAMP '9999-12-31 23:59:59.999999+00:00', with precision and time zone matching that specified for the valid-time data type.

UNTIL_CHANGED cannot be specified if the PERIOD is TIME.

Here' an example of inserting a row using UNTIL_CHANGED as the ending boundary.

```
INSERT INTO period_table VALUES
(2
,PERIOD(DATE'2011-09-26', UNTIL_CHANGED)
,PERIOD(TIME'11:22:33.44', TIME'11:33:33.44')
,PERIOD(TIME'09:09:09.000000+00:00',
TIME'10:10:10.000000+00:00')
,PERIOD(TIMESTAMP'2011-09-26 10:10:10.0000', UNTIL_CHANGED)
,PERIOD(TIMESTAMP'2011-09-26 12:34:56.123456+00:00',
UNTIL_CHANGED)
);

SELECT * FROM period_table WHERE c1 = 2;

 *** Query completed. One row found. 6 columns returned.
 *** Total elapsed time was 1 second.

c1           2
c2  ('11/09/26', '99/12/31')
c3  ('11:22:33.44', '11:33:33.44')
c4  ('09:09:09.000000+00:00', '10:10:10.000000+00:00')
c5  ('2011-09-26 10:10:10.0000', '9999-12-31 23:59:59.9999')
c6  ('2011-09-26 12:34:56.123456+00:00', '9999-12-31 23:59:59.999999+00:00')
```

Figure 14.5

AS OF Query

A SELECT . . . FROM . . . AS OF . . . statement extracts rows in temporal tables with overlapping valid-time and transaction-time periods. You can apply the AS OF clause to just the valid-time dimension, or just the transaction-time dimension, or both. It will return valid-time rows whose Period of Validity overlaps the AS OF time, and transaction-time rows with time periods that overlap the AS OF time. AS OF queries allow you to operate on a snapshot of data at any point in time, and are mostly used to query historical data.

There are differences between AS OF queries and current queries, as shown in the following figure.

CURRENT QUERIES	AS OF QUERIES
SELECT * FROM bitemporal;	**SELECT * FROM bitemporal AS OF <*datetime* exp>;**
Extracts rows based upon the current date and time when the query is submitted	Extracts rows based upon the specified *datetime*.
Only returns Open rows in the transaction-time dimension	Returns both Open and Closed transaction-time rows

Figure 14.6

Here's an example.

EXPLAIN
SELECT * FROM bitemporal AS OF CURRENT_DATE ORDER BY 1;

```
Explanation
-----------------------------------------------------------
  1) First, we lock a distinct CSQL_CLASS."pseudo table"
for read on a RowHash to prevent global deadlock for
CSQL_CLASS.bitemporal.
  2) Next, we lock CSQL_CLASS.bitemporal for read.
  3) We do an all-AMPs RETRIEVE step from
CSQL_CLASS.bitemporal (with temporal qualifier as
"VALIDTIME AS OF DATE '2013-04-03' AND TRANSACTIONTIME AS
OF DATE '2013-04-03'") by way of an all-rows scan with a
condition of ("((BEGIN(CSQL_CLASS.bitemporal.tracking
))<= TIMESTAMP '2013-04-03 00:00:00.000000+00:00') AND
(((END(CSQL_CLASS.bitemporal.dept_assign ))> DATE '2013-04-
03')AND (((BEGIN(CSQL_CLASS.bitemporal.dept_assign ))<=
DATE '2013-04-03') AND ((END(CSQL_CLASS.bitemporal.tracking
))> TIMESTAMP '2013-04-03 00:00:00.000000+00:00')))") into
Spool 1 (group_amps), which is built locally on the AMPs.
Then we do a SORT to order Spool 1 by the sort key in spool
field1.  The size of Spool 1 is estimated with no
confidence to be 7 rows (266 bytes). The estimated time for
this step is 0.03 seconds.
  4) Finally, we send out an END TRANSACTION step to all
AMPs involved in processing the request.
  -> The contents of Spool 1 are sent back to the user as
the result of statement 1.  The total estimated time is
0.03 seconds.
```

Figure 14.7

The following table describes the various temporal qualifiers that can be used with the DELETE, INSERT, SELECT, and UPDATE statements.

TEMPORAL QUALIFIER	**Description**
CURRENT VALID TIME This is the default if no other temporal qualifier is used.	The CURRENT VALIDTIME qualifier is used to qualify rows from the referenced tables in the valid-time dimension. In the transaction-time dimension, open rows qualify.
VALIDTIME AS OF *date_timestamp_expression*	A given time that must overlap the valid time of a row for that row to participate
VALIDTIME [*period_expression*]	The VALIDTIME or SEQUENCED VALIDTIME qualifier is used to qualify rows from the referenced tables in the valid-time dimension. In the transaction-time dimension, open rows qualify. The *period_expression* is the period of applicability.
SEQUENCED VALIDTIME [*period_expression*]	The VALIDTIME or SEQUENCED VALIDTIME qualifier is used to qualify rows from the referenced tables in the valid-time dimension. In the transaction-time dimension, open rows qualify. The *period_expression* is the period of applicability.
NONSEQUENCED VALIDTIME [*period_expression*]	The NONSEQUENCED VALIDTIME qualifier is used to qualify rows from the referenced tables in the

	valid-time dimension. In the transaction-time dimension, open rows qualify. The *period_expression* is the period of applicability.
NONTEMPORAL	The operation is nonsequenced in the valid-time dimension and nontemporal in the transaction-time dimension. The target table must support transaction time.
CURRENT TRANSACTIONTIME	The query is current in the transaction-time dimension. At least one table referenced in the operation, including tables or views or derived tables mentioned in the FROM clause of a subquery, must be a table that supports transaction time.
NONSEQUENCED TRANSACTIONTIME	The operation is nonsequenced in the transaction-time dimension. In a nonsequenced operation, the system does not associate any special meaning to the transaction-time column. The operation can use the transaction-time column like any other column. At least one table referenced in the operation, including tables or views or derived tables mentioned in the

	FROM clause of a subquery, must be a table that supports transaction time.
TRANSACTIONTIME AS OF *date_timestamp_expression*	The operation is AS OF in the transaction-time dimension. At least one table referenced in the operation, including tables or views or derived tables mentioned in the FROM clause of a subquery, must be a table that supports transaction time.

Figure 14.8

The next table matches the previous qualifiers to their respective DML statement(s).

TEMPORAL QUALIFIER	**DEL**	**INS**	**UPD**	**SEL**
CURRENT VALID TIME	Y	Y	Y	Y
VALIDTIME AS OF *date_timestamp_expression*				Y
VALIDTIME [*period_expression*]	Y	Y	Y	Y
SEQUENCED VALIDTIME [*period_expression*]	Y	Y	Y	Y
NONSEQUENCED VALIDTIME [*period_expression*]	Y	Y	Y	Y
NONTEMPORAL	Y	Y	Y	
CURRENT TRANSACTIONTIME				Y
NONSEQUENCED TRANSACTIONTIME				Y
TRANSACTIONTIME AS OF *date_timestamp_expression*				Y

Figure 14.9

Chapter 14: Practice Questions

1. What is the ending bound for the following PERIOD definition?

   PERIOD(DATE '2013-01-01' DATE '2013-02-01')

   a. January 30
   b. January 31
   c. February 1
   d. February 2

2. What is the DateTime granule for TIME(3)?
   a. One tenth of a second
   b. One hundredth of a second
   c. One thousandth of a second
   d. One ten thousandth of a second

3. Which of the following PERIOD expressions is invalid?
   a. PERIOD(DATE'2013-01-01', UNTIL_CHANGED)
   b. PERIOD(TIME'10:10:10', UNTIL_CHANGED)
   c. PERIOD(TIMESTAMP'2011-11-11 01:02:03, UNTIL_CHANGED)
   d. PERIOD(TIMESTAMP'2012-12-12 12:12:12.123456', UNTIL_CHANGED)

4. Which DML statement cannot be used with the NONTEMPORAL qualifier?
   a. Delete
   b. Insert
   c. Select
   d. Update

5. Which of the following temporal qualifiers can only be used with the SELECT statement?
    a. CURRENT VALID TIME
    b. SEQUENCED VALIDTIME
    c. VALIDTIME
    d. VALIDTIME AS OF

Chapter Notes

Utilize this space for notes, key points to remember, diagrams, areas of further study, etc.

Chapter 15: Compression

Certification Objectives

- ✓ Describe table-level options.
- ✓ Given a scenario, determine the most effective columns available for compression.
- ✓ Given a scenario, identify when to use a non-compressed join index vs. a compressed join index.
- ✓ Identify the column level compression options (e.g., Multivalued compression (MVC) and algorithmic Compression (ALC).
- ✓ Identify the table level compression options (e.g., Block Level Compression (BLC) and Temperature-based Block Level Compression (TBBLC)).
- ✓ Identify the techniques to determine candidate columns for Multivalued compression (MVC).

Before You Begin

You should be familiar with the following terms and concepts.

Terms	Key Concepts
Multi-Value Compression	Considerations and rules for implementation
Data Types	What can be Compressed
Table Row Header	Calculating overhead for Compression

Compression allows multiple values to be compressed, up to 255 distinct values plus NULL. By employing this technique, you have the ability to reduce table storage sizes and spool space consumption.

Depending on the query submitted, compression often results in improved response times by reducing I/O and possibly CPU consumption. While improved storage capacity can be immediately and easily recognized, it is more difficult to measure the performance improvements without a thorough test plan.

Compression enables more rows to be stored per physical block, resulting in less overall blocks to store and process data as compression is carried through spool operations. In turn, this means less work is required during a query operation. Disk I/O is further reduced because the compressed values are more likely to be memory resident and don't require disk access. Compression may improve I/O consumption for full table scans providing a performance benefit.

The best candidates for compression are columns with a low or small number of distinct values. Even though these column characteristics are the very best candidates, you may choose to compress other columns just to save space. This is perfectly legitimate.

Here are some general rules and facts about compression:

- Up to 255 values can be compressed per column, including NULL values.
- You can't compress primary index columns.
- You can't compress volatile or derived table columns.
- You can't compress referencing foreign key columns.
- Nulls are automatically compressed when the COMPRESS clause is assigned.
- Compression is case sensitive.

You can perform multi-value compression only for the following types of data:

- Nulls
- Zeros

- Blanks
- Constants having any of the following data types:
  - BYTE (up to 510 bytes)
  - VARBYTE (up to 510 bytes per value)
  - CHARACTER (up to 510 characters per value)
  - VARCHAR (up to 510 characters per value)
  - DATE (expressed as COMPRESS (DATE 'yyyy-mm-dd'))
  - Any numeric data type

How Compression Works

Compression values are defined at the column level. The CREATE/ALTER (DDL) table statement is used to identify the column values that will be compressed. When implemented, compressed values are moved out of the row and stored in the table header once. No matter how many times this value repeats itself at the row level, it is only stored once in the table header.

The first 14 bytes of every table row header is reserved for overhead. Presence bytes are used for both nullability and compression. An extra presence bit is needed when a column is defined as nullable. Even if there is no compression defined on the column, one presence bit will be required if the column is defined as nullable. If a null value is stored in this non-compressed and nullable column, then the presence bit will contain a 0.

Teradata uses the binary interpretation of the presence bits to index the compression values. Any values that are not compressed and NOT NULL will have all zeroes for their presence bits. If the column is defined as nullable, then compressible values will start with a leading 0 presence bit and will contain at least one 1 in the rest of the presence bits. Values that don't get compressed will start with a 1 as the leading presence bit, and the rest of its presence bits will be 0.

The example below shows a table that has compression on the Dept_No column. This column is also defined to allow for NULL values because the NOT NULL has not been specified.

```
CREATE SET TABLE csql_class.employee_table_comprx
( Employee_no INTEGER
, Last_name  CHAR(20)
, First_name VARCHAR(12)
, Salary  DECIMAL (8,2)
, Dept_no  SMALLINT COMPRESS (200, 300, 400, 500)
)
UNIQUE PRIMARY INDEX (Employee_no)
INDEX (Dept_no) ;
```

Figure 15.1

The illustration below demonstrates how presence bit patterns are defined on the compressed table. Notice that values with leading "0's" followed by a combination of "0's" and "1's" are compressed. Also, values with leading "1's" followed by all "0's" are not compressed in the table row header. In addition, note that the NULLs are represented by all "0's". The leading "0" or "1" indicates that the column is nullable.

This leading bit would not be required if the column was not NULL.

Table Header

Employee_No INTEGER	Last_Name CHAR(20)	Dept_No SMALLINT COMPRESS

Presen ce Bits	Dept_No
0000	NULL
0001	200
0010	300
0011	400
0100	500

Data Rows

Presence Bits	Employee_No	Last_Name	Dept_No
0001	112346	Jones	
0010	145678	Smith	
0011	098876	Richards	
0010	334562	Willis	
1000	556321	Nelson	600
0100	776541	Rex	
0001	889121	Reiter	
0000	743465	Lee	

Figure 15.2

As you can see, all the combinations of bit patterns are used to identify and locate the values. In this example, the bit patterns and their corresponding values are listed below:

- 0000-Rows where Dept_No is NULL
- 0001-Dept_No = 200 is compressed in the table header
- 0010-Dept_No = 300 is compressed in the table header
- 0011-Dept_No = 400 is compressed in the table header
- 0100-Dept_No = 500 is compressed in the table header
- 1000-Dept_NO = 600 is NOT compressed in the table header

In this case, there are 5 potential values for compression (NULL, 200, 300, 400, 500), which requires 4 bits because the column is nullable.

These values will be stored in the table row header. However, only Dept_No 600 will be stored in the base row.

Determining the Table Header Size

To determine how much table header size is being taken up by compression, you can get a rough idea by creating two tables, one with compression and one without. Leaving both tables empty, query the catalog with the following query:

```
SELECT TableName, CurrentPerm
FROM DBC.TableSize
WHERE DatabaseName = 'csql_class'
AND TableName IN ('Employee_table', 'Employee_table_comprx') ;
```

Figure 15.3

The above query will return a single row for each table and for every AMP on the system. This is because table header information, or CREATE TABLE definition, is stored on all AMPs. Even if an AMP has no rows located on it, they will still have the compressed values stored in the table header. With this approach, it is actually possible to use more space with compression turned on. However, if each AMP contains the compressed value at least once, then compression should be saving space. As the frequency of the values increase in the table, the space savings increases proportionately.

Lastly, since the compressed values are stored in the table header row, the CREATE/ALTER statement will fail if adding the compress values for a column causes the table row header to exceed 1MB, which is the maximum size. The table header will either require 64KB (a thin header) or 1MB (a fat header).

Considerations Before Implementing Compression

Before implementing compression, make sure you consider possible alternatives first. There are several techniques that can save space before compression is implemented. For example, make sure your data types are as narrow as possible first. This will save space before compression is applied.

In order to do this correctly, you need to know how many bytes are taken up by each data type and implement them as efficiently as possible. For example, if you code INTEGER for a column that never contains values greater than 100, then you are wasting space. Integers use up 4 bytes. Utilizing a BYTEINT instead for this column would have sufficed and only used up a single byte. When applied, these techniques can provide significant space savings before the implementation of compression.

Take note that VARCHAR uses two bytes for every column and every row. Actually, the first VARCHAR column in the CREATE TABLE statement uses four bytes of overhead, and every VARCHAR in the row after that consumes two bytes just for overhead. Therefore, never code VARCHAR(1) as a data type. CHAR(1) will always use less space. This is true whether you define compression on this column or not. Considerable space savings may be gained simply by changing VARCHAR to CHAR for certain columns.

Determining the Proper Data Type

As noted previously, make sure you have the most efficient field widths first. The following SQL or function (TYPE) demonstrates how to determine the correct data type. Perform the following function call on the maximum value expected for a given column:

```
SELECT TYPE(102.98) ;
Answer: DECIMAL(5,2)

SELECT TYPE(10998) ;
Answer:  SMALLINT
```

Figure 15.4

Implementing Compression

After identifying the list of compressed values for each column, they are defined in the CREATE TABLE statement. You can implement compression with the CREATE statement, or in some cases, with the ALTER table statement. Here is an example of the syntax on Dept_No:

```
CREATE SET TABLE csql_class.employee_table_new
( Employee_no INTEGER
, Last_name  CHAR(20)
, First_name VARCHAR(12)
, Salary  DECIMAL (8,2)
, Dept_no  SMALLINT COMPRESS (200, 300, 400, 500, 600)
)
UNIQUE PRIMARY INDEX (Employee_no)
INDEX (Dept_no) ;
```

Figure 15.5

Note: An alternative approach is to create a copy of the original table with the new compression clauses in place. From there, you insert the data, collect statistics, and replace/rename this table with the current table.

Compression savings are a function of the number of values compressed, the frequency that those values appear in the table and the field width. Table header limits are more easily reached when the fields are wider. Therefore, you will want to take the Top N values for these wider columns. This may be desired for other columns as well just to maintain the readability of the DDL.

We mentioned that you can compress up to 255 values per column, but that doesn't mean you should. Typically, the number of optimal column values to compress is less than 255 values. This is based on the data that is stored in the table. In addition, you may choose to compress fewer values in order to maintain the readability of the DDL, which might be an important consideration when implementing compression.

Note: Assignment of default values on the columns, like zero for numeric or blank for character defined columns, should also be considered as compression candidate values.

Another best practice when optimizing value compression is to ensure column values do not exceed the size of the row header maximum size. Keep the number of values within these boundaries (1, 3, 7, 15, 31, 63, 127, or 255) because these numbers of values will not require additional presence bits in the row header. However, if enough columns use additional presence bit(s), this will require a longer row header. In this case, having fewer values is sometimes better if it does not require additional presence bytes, so you may need to test different scenarios.

Compression Case Sensitivity Example

We also mentioned that compression is case sensitive even though Teradata, by default, is not. This requires a work-around when data being inserted is of mixed case. The following example will shed some light on this issue.

```
CREATE SET TABLE csql_class.employee_table
( Employee_no INTEGER
, Last_name  CHAR(20) COMPRESS 'Flintstone'
, First_name VARCHAR(12)
, Salary  DECIMAL (8,2)
, Dept_no  SMALLINT COMPRESS (200, 300, 400, 500, 600)
)
UNIQUE PRIMARY INDEX (Employee_no)
INDEX (Dept_no) ;
```

Figure 15.6

In this example, we are now compressing Last_name for values of 'Flintstone'. However, if 'FLINTSTONE' is inserted into the table, compression will not take place. This is fixed with the UPPERCASE keyword as the following syntax illustrates:

```
, Last_name CHAR(20) COMPRESS 'FLINTSTONE' UPPERCASE
```

Figure 15.7

This will now compress both 'Flintstone' and 'FLINTSTONE' or any other combination of upper and lower case when rows are inserted into the table because it is forced to upper case. The downside of this alternative is that all values will get returned as UPPERCASE when retrieved.

Alter Options with Compression

You can use the ALTER TABLE command to add a new column with multi-value compression to an existing table, add multi-value compression to an existing column, or drop compression from an existing column. Use the NO COMPRESS attribute to drop compression from a column. If a column is defined as NOT NULL, then the compression list cannot contain the literal NULL.

The ALTER TABLE COMPRESS syntax supports the following:

- Both populated and empty tables
- Global Temporary tables
- Base table columns where join indexes are defined
- Base table columns where hash indexes are defined

To ALTER a table in order to add compression columns, use the ALTER TABLE option as shown below:

```
ALTER TABLE csql_class.Employee_table
ADD gender CHAR(6) COMPRESS ('Female', 'Male') ,
ADD job_desc CHAR(20) COMPRESS ('Manager', 'Supervisor',
'Programmer') ;
```

Figure 15.8

The ALTER statement can also compress populated columns. This is implemented by using the ALTER TABLE MODIFY option as shown below.

```
ALTER TABLE csql_class.employee_table
MODIFY dept_no
COMPRESS (200, 300, 400, 500, 600, 700, 800) ;
```

Figure 15.9

Take note that this command will enforce an exclusive lock on the table for the entire duration of the command. This could have a significant impact if the table is large because users will be unable to read or write to this table while this compress operation is taking place. Therefore, if you are working with large tables, it is recommended that you do these types of operations during off-hours.

Compressed Join Indexes

Join Index compression is a form of logical data compression in which Teradata Database stores a repeating column value set only once, while any non-repeating column values that belong to that set are stored as logical extensions of the base repeating set. Row compression is a lossless method. This form of compression is a feature of Join Indexes.

In the following example, the join index JI_NRC does not specify any row compression, while the join index JI_RC identifies the first two columns should have duplicate values compressed.

```
CREATE JOIN INDEX JI_NRC AS
SELECT c1, c2, c3, c4, c5
FROM tbl_10
PRIMARY INDEX (c3);

CREATE JOIN INDEX JI_RC AS
SELECT (c1, c2), (c3, c4, c5)
FROM tbl_12
PRIMARY INDEX (c3);
```

Figure 15.10

Like multi-value compression, there is no decompression necessary to access row compressed data values. You control the row compression of join indexes with the syntax you use when you create an index. The row compression of hash indexes is automatic and requires no special syntax.

Column Compression

With column partitioning, the system has various system-applied compression techniques that it can employ automatically to reduce storage requirements. As with all compression methodologies, these can reduce the I/O required to process queries. If they are combined with row partitioning, the number of compression opportunities might increase.

The system chooses which autocompression to use on a container-by-container basis. It all depends upon the context.

The most common way to load rows into a column-partitioned or unpartitioned NoPI table is to use an INSERT/SELECT statement. Whenever you have a target table that does not have a primary index, you can specify the HASH BY and LOCAL ORDER BY clauses to distribute and sort rows coming from the source table. These options can be specified individually or together in the request.

The HASH BY <*column_name_list*> redistributes rows by the hash value of the column(s) you specify. This option is useful if the output of the INSERT / SELECT doesn't provide even distribution.

If the target table is column-partitioned, you can follow the HASH BY clause with a LOCAL ORDER BY <*column_name_list*> which will sort the rows locally and then insert them into the target table (or the underlying table of the target view). Through these two options, you can distribute equal values of a column to the same AMP which may improve autocompression of the column(s) you use to calculate the hash value.

To disable autocompression, specify NO AUTO COMPRESSION, otherwise the system applies autocompression automatically. Using NO AUTO COMMPRESSION prevents the system from applying autocompression to the physical rows. The system will still apply any other user-specified compression, such as Multivalued Compression (MVC) and Algorithmic Compression (ALC).

Algorithmic Compression

This option is defined at the column level, just like Multivalued Compression, and is normally specified on the CREATE TABLE but can be added, removed or changed using an ALTER TABLE statement.

Algorithmic Compression (ALC) is implemented using User Defined Functions (UDFs). For each column that is compressed using the ALC feature, you specify or create two UDF's, one to compress the data upon storage, and one to decompress the data upon retrieval.

Unlike Multivalued compression, the decompression UDF must be executed every time the system has to read a data value that has been compressed using ALC, even if the row is subsequently discarded. Since this effort requires additional CPU cycles, make your decompression UDF as efficient as possible.

ALC can only be applied to columns with the following data types:

BYTE	VARBYTE
CHARACTER	VARCHAR
GRAPHIC	VARGRAPHIC
All Period types except for VALIDTIME and TRANSACTIONTIME columns	All non-LOB-based UDT types

Figure 15.11

Implementing Algorithmic Compression

The following SQL is an example of specifying ALC for a column in a table.

```
CREATE TABLE Employee_Table
(employee_no INTEGER
,last_name CHAR(20) COMPRESS USING udfCOMPRESS
            DECOMPRESS USING udfDECOMPRESS
,first_name VARCHAR(20)
,salary DECIMAL(8,2)
)
UNIQUE PRIMARY INDEX(employee_no);
```

Figure 15.12

In performing a CREATE TABLE command, the system validates the existence of any UDFs referenced and verifies their parameters are compatible with the column's data type. The compress and decompress UDFs must be in either the SYSUDTLIB or TD_SYSFNLIB database. The TD_SYSFNLIB is for internal use and should not be used to store the UDFs you write

ALC and MVC can co-exist for the same column. The following SQL example is valid.

```
CREATE TABLE Employee_Table
(employee_no INTEGER
,last_name CHAR(20) COMPRESS ('SMITH','JONES')
          COMPRESS USING udfCOMPRESS
          DECOMPRESS USING udfDECOMPRESS
,FIrst_name VARCHAR(20)
,salary DECIMAL(8,2)
)
UNIQUE PRIMARY INDEX(employee_no);
```

Figure 15.13

With this definition in place, if rows are added or updated so that the value for column last_name is 'SMITH' or 'JONES' (which is case-sensitive) then the column will be compressed using MVC. Any other values will be passed to the 'udfCOMPRESS' routine and the output from that routine will be physically stored in the data row.

Though ALC and MVC can be specified for the same column, the names of the UDFs used for algorithmic compression are stored in the table header and in the COMPRESSVALUELIST column for DBC.TVFIELDS. Therefore, adding ALC will reduce the number of MVC values you can specify.

Software-Based Block-Level Compression

Block Level Compression (BLC) is specified at the table level, and not at the column level like Join Index Row Compression, Multivalued Compression, and Algorithmic Compression.

If BLC is specified for a table, then whenever a data block is to be written to disk, the BLC routine tests to see if "enough" space can be compressed to make it worth the overhead. If so, then the block is compressed and written to disk. If not, then the uncompressed block is written to disk. There are control fields in the DBSCONTROL record which determine how much compression is "enough". These control field values apply to all tables using Block Level Compression.

Implementing Block-Level Compression

Block Level Compression can be implemented for a table using one of two methods.

- For all existing data in a table, use the Ferret utility. Once BLC is enabled, all future data blocks will be tested for compression before being written to disk.

- Use the Teradata QUERYBAND feature when loading new data. This tells the system that any data blocks which are updated or built during the execution of this script should be tested for compression.

The following SQL shows how to set the QUERYBAND for BLC.

```
SET QUERY_BAND = 'BlockCompression=Yes;' FOR SESSION;
```

Figure 15.14

Temperature-Based Block-Level Compression

HOT, WARM, COLD. These temperature ratings are maintained by Teradata Virtual Storage in determining what can be compressed. Data that is rarely accessed (COLD) and data that is occasionally accessed (WARM) might be compressed automatically, while data that is frequently accessed (HOT) might end up being automatically decompressed if it was previously compressed.

The BLOCKCOMPRESSION option of the CREATE TABLE statement controls the table's temperature-based block-level compression, based upon the following option values.

- AUTOTEMP – The temperature state can be changed by the file system at any time based on its TVS statistical temperature.
- DEFAULT – Compression is controlled by the DBSCONTROL parameter DefaultTableMode.
- MANUAL – Compression is not managed automatically.
- NEVER – Block level compression is completely turned off. This is true even if a QUERYBAND or DBSCONTROL parameter default specifies otherwise.

TVS keeps track of the temperature metrics at the cylinder level when BLC in turned on. TVS takes all temperatures into account when it determines what data is associated with what temperature. Temperature-based block-level compression only applies to permanent user data tables.

Compression Considerations

The following rules apply when adding or modifying rows with compression:

1. For single-value compression, the default for the compress value is NULL.
2. There is no default for multi-value compression. All values in the compression list must be specified explicitly.
3. NULL does not need to be specified in a multi-value compression statement. If there is a COMPRESS clause, NULL is compressed automatically.

4. You can modify an existing column to have multi-value compression.
5. You cannot add a compress value to a column if the table header row exceeds its maximum length of 1 MB for Teradata Version 13 & 14.

You should not compress columns where NULL values are subject to change. If NULL values change, the column will expand and you could cause block splits. Additional considerations include:

- Adding a column that is not compressible will most likely expand all rows.
- Adding a column that is compressible where there are no spare presence bits will expand the row size.
- Nullable fields also require a presence bit, even if it is not compressible. Therefore, if there are no spare presence bits, the row header and each row will expand.
- Dropping a column changes all row sizes where data is present.

Chapter 15: Practice Questions

1. Into which database should compress/decompress UDFs be placed?
    a. SYSUDTLIB
    b. SQLJ
    c. SYSLIB
    d. SYSSPATIAL

2. Choose the correct syntax to have join index row compression applied to the first three columns.
    a. CREATE JOIN INDEX jx_1 AS
       SELECT (C1, C2, C3), C4, C4 FROM T1
       PRIMARY INDEX C4;
    b. CREATE JOIN INDEX jx_1 AS
       SELECT (C1, C2, C3), (C4, C4) FROM T1
       PRIMARY INDEX C4;
    c. CREATE JOIN INDEX jx_1 AS
       SELECT (C1, C2), C3, C4, C4 FROM T1
       PRIMARY INDEX C4;
    d. CREATE JOIN INDEX jx_1 AS
       SELECT (C1, C2, C3, C4, C4) FROM T1
       PRIMARY INDEX C4;

3. What is the maximum size a CHAR column value can be for compression?
    a. 128 bytes
    b. 255 bytes
    c. 510 bytes
    d. 512 bytes

4. Which of the following can be compressed?
    a. Primary index columns
    b. Volatile table columns
    c. Derived table columns
    d. Referencing foreign key columns
    e. Nulls

5. To use the HASH BY and LOCAL ORDER BY clauses to distribute and sort the rows from the SELECT subquery of an INSERT ... SELECT request, the target table must be a ____ or a ______. (Choose 2)
    a. Column partitioned SET table
    b. NoPI SET table
    c. UPI MULTISET table
    d. NoPI MULTISET table
    e. Column partitioned MULTISET table

Chapter Notes

Utilize this space for notes, key points to remember, diagrams, areas of further study, etc.

Chapter 16: Statistics

Certification Objectives

- ✓ Describe the tables and views used for Statistics Collection.
- ✓ Determine when multi-column statistics are useful.
- ✓ Given a scenario, describe conditions where stale stats can impact performance.
- ✓ Given a scenario, identify columns that are appropriate for statistics collection.
- ✓ Identify the utilities available to determine which statistics are useful.
- ✓ Identify how ROLLUP Optimization can improve collect times.
- ✓ Identify when MAXINTERVALS are useful.
- ✓ Identify when SAMPLE statistics are sufficient.
- ✓ Identify when SUMMARY statistics are sufficient.
- ✓ Interpret the output of SHOW and HELP STATISTICS statements.

Before You Begin

You should be familiar with the following terms and concepts.

Terms	Key Concepts
Statistics Options	What are the different methods for collecting Stats
Collecting Stats	Best practices for deploying Statistics
Multi-Column Stats	Considerations for when to utilize for performance
Data Dictionary	How does this impact Statistics

Statistics are a critical component in ensuring the Optimizer chooses a good query plan when SQL statements are submitted for processing. There are three approaches to collecting statistics which are as follows:

1. Random (Dynamic) AMP Sampling
2. Full statistics collection
3. Using the SAMPLE option

Collecting stats provides the Optimizer with a row count in the table(s) being queried. The Optimizer will then utilize this formation to determine the best way to access the data. The benefits of collecting stats are as follows:

- If your data distribution is uneven, then stats can improve in accessing a column or index data during a query operation.
- Statistics provide the Optimizer the ability to use a secondary, hash, or join indexes as opposed to doing full-table scans in queries.
- Provide performance benefits when doing complex queries and joins operations.
- Improve the estimates of intermediate spool files based on the conditions specified in an SQL query. This is critical for determining join order for tables along with identifying the type of join to best resolve query.
- Empower the Optimizer to take advantage of NUSI Bit Mapping when available.
- Statistics information remains intact during reconfiguration operations.

Collect Statistics Process

During the stats collection process, Teradata will collect and process data demographic information on each AMP. Once complete, this information is sent to one AMP in order to merge, sort, and distribute the data based on the frequency into 250 intervals.

Depending on the distribution and the degree of skew in the data for each column, there are three histogram options that can be utilized to determine the cardinality and statistics:

1. Equally distributed and height interval histogram. This means that each of the 250 intervals has the same number of values. For this to happen, the widths in the intervals must vary.

2. 250 equal-height intervals in the histogram. This states that intervals represent a percentile for the values it represents.

3. For each column, statistics are expressed as an equal-height no skewing interval histogram if the frequencies of its values are normally distributed.

Note: The maximum number of intervals can be configure for 500.

Each interval consists of roughly .4% of the table rows. The information gathered on the table consists of the following:

- Most frequent data value for the column or index.
- Number of rows with the most frequent data value.
- Number of data values not equal to the most frequent data value.
- Number of rows not equal to the most frequent data value.
- The minimum data value for the table.
- Number of NULLs.

The AMPs will either do a full table scan or a SAMPLE depending on which Collect Statistics command is utilized.

The employee table has 100,000 rows and statistics are collected on the dept_no column. These values are gathered in 200 intervals with 500 rows in each. When queries are processed using the dept_no column, the Optimizer can better estimate on how many rows the AMPs will have to retrieve to complete the SQL query. The following diagram is an example of the statistics gathered:

Interval	Max Value	Most Frequent Value	Most Frequent Rows	Other Values	Other Rows
1	1001	1007	175	41	976
2	1259	1178	185	56	865
3	1560	1347	250	79	754
:	:	:	:	:	:
97	1875	1657	345	123	865
:	:	:	:	:	:

Figure 16.1

STATS Storage

Table-level and single column statistics for a table are stored in DBC.StatsTbl. Statistics for indexes and composite column sets are stored in DBC.Indexes.

Composite column sets are treated as pseudoindexes, and it doesn't make any difference whether you collect statistics as an INDEX set or a COLUMN set, the statistics are still stored in DBC.Indexes. Pseudoindexes are assigned their own set of unique ID numbers and therefore do not reduce the number of indexes you can define on a table. Pseudoindexes have the same limits as regular indexes. That means you cannot define more than 64 columns for a column set, and cannot collect statistics on more than 32 composite column sets.

Statistics Considerations

There is a limit of 512 columns and indexes for a single table that you can collect or refresh statistics on. Though this may consume more resources to accomplish, you gain the benefit of better query plans that will consume fewer resources. Do not collect statistics on columns not referenced in queries since this uses system resources without providing any performance gains.

There are five primary areas in where statistics should be collected.

1. Tables
2. Columns
3. Multi-Columns
4. Indexes
5. Partitions

For single-column indexes, collect statistics at the COLUMN level since indexes can be dropped and recreated frequently.

You need the STATISTICS privilege to collect statistics. You can use the HELP STATS command, shown later in this chapter, to review the statistics collected on a table.

You can collect statistics on Global Temporary Tables, but when the user logs off, the data and statistics for the table are deleted.

Multi-Column Statistics Considerations

If a frequently used access path (indexed or not) consists of multiple ANDed columns, collecting statistics on the individual columns will not help the Optimizer. The optimizer needs to know what the combined mix of values looks like:

```
SELECT * FROM tname
WHERE col10 = 100 AND col12 = 'abc' ;

        --- or ---

CREATE INDEX (col10, col12) ON tname;
```

Figure 16.2

Multi-Column Statistics Considerations include:

- Order of columns within the collected statistics will be the same order as in the CREATE TABLE statement.
- Gives the optimizer information about correlations among columns of the same table.
- Provides better estimates if a query has constraints on more than 1 column of a table.
- Query constraints must be in an equal condition.
- Default formulas are used if the query expresses non-equal conditions.
- Interval "Values" are limited to 25 Bytes for single columns and 30 Bytes for multi-columns. Any values that exceed this may be truncated.
- The full-length value is collected and reflected in Interval Zero, but Max, Mode in detail Intervals are truncated at 25 or 30 Bytes.
- If multiple values share the same 25 or 30 Byte high-order string, optimizer cannot distinguish among them.
- When VARCHAR columns are present they are converted to full length before statistics collection.
- Best when Varchar columns appear last in multicolumn statistics.
- Nulls in multi-column statistics.
- Histogram interval 0 has two columns for NULLs:

  - Number of Nulls – Count of all rows which have NULL on any or all columns.
  - Number of all Nulls – Count of rows which have NULL on all columns.
- Can derive number of rows with "Partial NULLs".
- Number of Nulls minus Number of all Nulls.
- Multi-Column Statistics with NULLs may result in an over-count of Distinct Values when there is a high number of partial NULLs.
- Evaluate collecting multi-column statistics when one or more columns have NULLs by testing if it is helping the queries or not.

Notes:

- Each column in a multi-column statistic will by default get 30 Bytes for the statistics collection process, and then have 25 Bytes of space for each separate value to be represented in the histogram. This means each column in a multi-column statistic will have its first 25 Bytes displayed instead of truncated at 16 Bytes from the beginning of the combined string, as was the case in earlier Teradata Releases.

- Secondary index columns may qualify for NUSI Bit Mapping with individual statistics being available.

Random AMP Sampling

Random AMP Sampling (a.k.a. Dynamic Sampling) uses the Table Id to choose an AMP to get statistics. Using the Table Id prevents one AMP from being overloaded with sampling requests. Since the default is to sample only one AMP, if the data on the selected AMP isn't evenly distributed, the Optimizer could make inefficient choices. With

Dynamic Sampling, the Optimizer will always choose a conservative path.

There are two internal flags that control Dynamic Sampling.

- You can change the number of AMPs to use for sampling. As an example, you can specify 2 AMPs, or 5 AMPs, or more.
- You can control the percentage of rows to read.

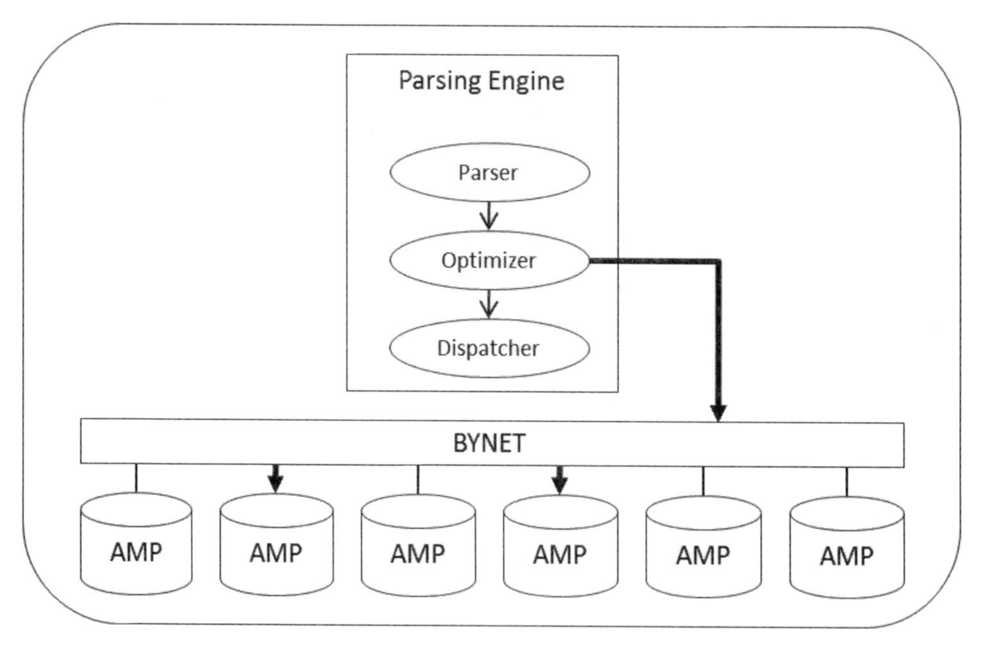

Figure 16.3

Dynamic AMP sampling calculates the average size of each index for every AMP based on the following criteria:

- Table cardinality
- The average cardinality per value
- The number of distinct values (indexes)
- The average cardinality for each index

Tables with heavily skewed data will improve greatly with this new option. Because of multiple AMP sampling, the Optimizer will receive better estimates when generating query plans.

Data Dictionary Cache

The dictionary cache is a buffer in parsing engine memory that stores the most recently used dictionary information. These entries, which also contain statistical information, are used by the Optimizer to convert database object names to their numeric IDs.

Caching the information reduces the I/O activity for the following items:

- Resolving database object names
- Optimizing access paths
- Validating access rights

When the Parser needs definitions not found in cache, it asks an AMP to retrieve the necessary information. After the information is received, the Parser stores it in the dictionary cache. If another SQL statement requires information about the same database object, the Parser retrieves it from cache rather than performing the more costly task of asking the AMP multiple times for the same information.

If an SQL statement changes the contents of the data dictionary, a spoil message is sent to every PE, instructing them to drop the changed definitions from their respective dictionary caches. The dictionary cache is purged periodically, phased so that the cache for only one PE is purged at a time.

Full Statistics

A full COLLECT STATISTICS statement is the most complete method of gathering demographic information about a column or an index. Below are the benefits:

- Best option for columns or indexes where data is highly skewed.
- Recommended for small tables, with fewer than 100 rows per AMP.
- Columns where the number of distinct values is moderate or low.
- For all NUSIs and other access columns used with queries.
- For all columns/indexes where the USING SAMPLE does not provide accurate estimates.

Statistics can now be collected on global temporary tables; however, there is still no support for volatile tables. In order to get as accurate a row count as possible, the more extensive dynamic AMP sampling approach, that samples all AMPs, is used by default for volatile tables.

Because tables are in a constant state of change, it is up to the administrator to keep collected statistics refreshed. It is common practice for many Teradata sites to re-collect statistics on the majority of their tables, or partitions, when they change by 10%.

Sample Statistics

Full table statistics requires scanning the base table in order to sort, and calculate the number of occurrences for each distinct value. The process in some case can be time consuming and the resources required to collect and refresh statistics can create problems especially on large tables.

Using the sample option reduces the resources and time required to perform statistics collection. This should not be utilized as a replacement for full statistics collection. It is recommended that analysis and planning should be conducted utilizing this option. Sampling is recommended for the following:

- Large tables.
- Resource consumption from the collection process is a serious performance or cost concern.

Sampling is not recommended for the following:

- Small tables.
- To replace all existing full scan collections.
- If the system does not determine the correct sample size which will impact accurate statistics.
- Statistics on a column or index are either sample or full. It cannot be both and the when you refresh statistics, the system will determine if the stats are sample or full.
- Do not use sampling with highly skewed data.
- Multicolumn statistics with system-derived column PARTITION. A partitioning column is the table column referenced in the PARTITION BY clause.

Note: This feature cannot be utilized on global temporary tables or join indexes.

Summary Statistics

COLLECT SUMMARY STATISTICS specifies that only object-level statistical information be collected. This includes things such as average row size, average block size, one-AMP sampling estimates, all-AMP sampling estimates, and cardinality. SUMMARY statistics on unpartitioned tables are very useful to the Optimizer for making cardinality estimates.

If you submit a COLECT SUMMARY STATISTICS statement, it cannot contain any USING options, references, or explicit COLUMN or INDEX references. Also, you cannot specify SUMMARY for volatile tables.

The FROM option, along with the SUMMARY option, allows you to copy table-level demographics from the source table to the target table. Unless you specify the column list for both tables, the system implicitly copies the SUMMARY stats from the source table to the target table. If only summary statistics are copied to the target table, you should explicitly recollect the statistics on the target table later on.

COLLECT STATISTICS Detailed Syntax

The following diagram shows the Optimizer form of the COLLECT STATISTICS command.

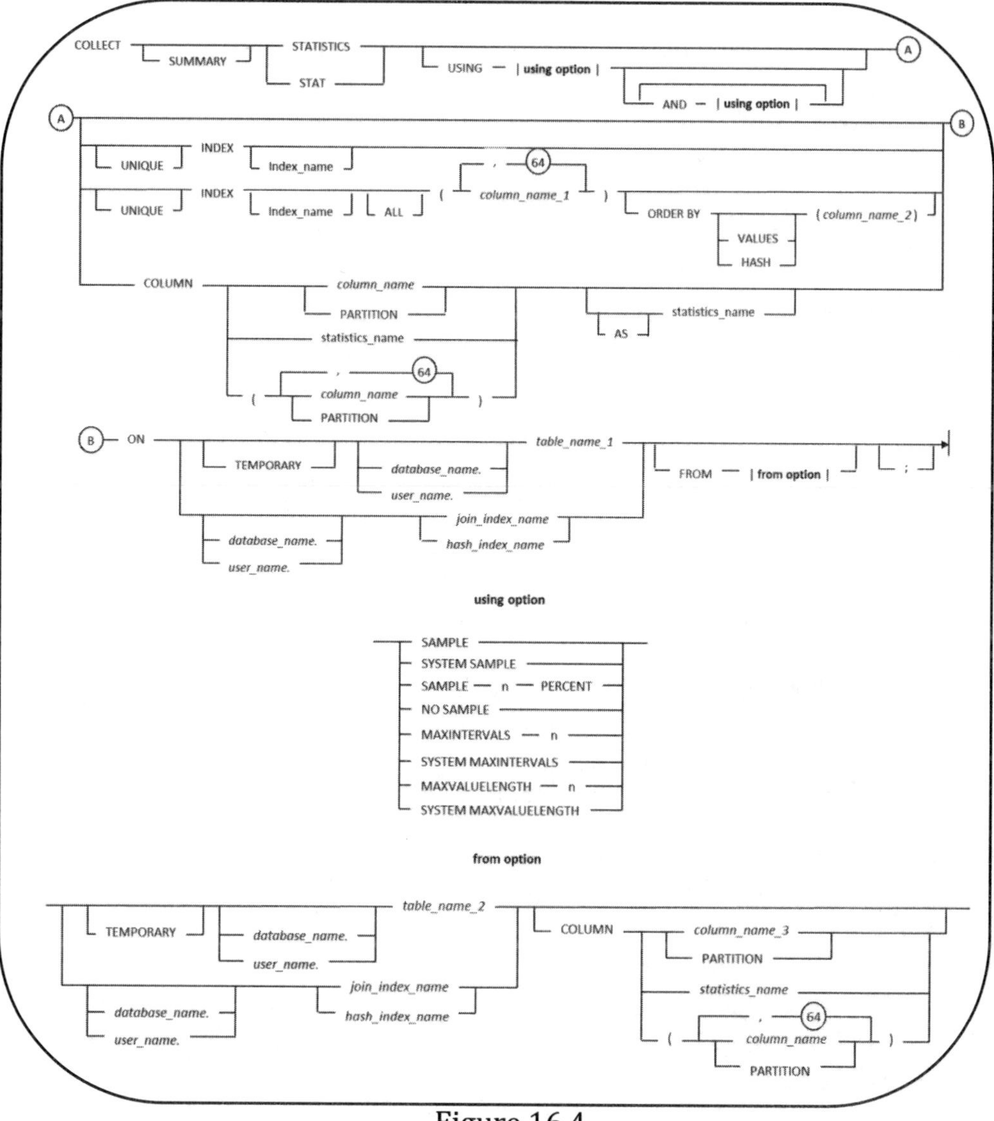

Figure 16.4

Keep in mind when using the SAMPLE option, the sample data size is a percentage of the total set of rows on a given AMP.

Full Statistics

The system always does a full table scan when it collects full statistics on a table. It also does a full index scan when it collects statistics on an index. The exception is when you collect statistics on the PARTITION and PARTITION#Ln columns. Obviously, the amount of time required to do the scans is dependent upon the size of the table, the configuration of the system, and the current workload.

In addition to the scan times, the system has to compute the statistical measures which summarize the characteristics of a column or index, and then create the histogram.

Unique indexes and columns which are not indexed take longer to process than NUSIs.

Through judicious use of the USING options, you can control the time it takes to collect or recollect statistics.

USING SAMPLE
USING SYSTEM SAMPLE
USING SAMPLE *n* PERCENT

Instead of collecting statistics on all of the rows or hoping that dynamic sampling will suffice, you can sample a subset of table rows instead.

The USING SAMPLE is only provided for backward compatibility, and is identical to the USING SYSTEM SAMPLE. You should use USING SYSTEM SAMPLE.

Here are some guidelines on using sampling.

- Use sampling if the column or index is unique or nearly unique.
- Use sampling if the table contains in excess of 10^{10} rows.
- Do not use sampling on small tables.
- You cannot use sampling to collect COLUMN statistics for single row partitioning columns.
- You should not use sampling to collect INDEX statistics for single row partitioning columns. I you try, the system will ignore your request and collect full statistics.
- You cannot collect less than 100% on the system-derived PARTITION column set. However, this collection only involves a scan of the cylinder indexes for the table plus *n*+1 data blocks, where *n* is the number of partitions in the table, so it is fairly fast.

The column SampleSizePct in the DBC.StatsTbl will show the sampling percentage used for any collection.

USING MAXINTERVALS *n*
USING SYSTEM MAXINTERVALS

The MAXINTERVALS *n* provides you with the ability to control how many histogram intervals the collected statistics should be placed into. The value you specify for *n* must be an integer number in the range of 0-500. If you state zero intervals, the system only captures summary level statistics. If you specify a value greater than zero, the system might adjust the value up or down depending on the maximum histogram size.

By requesting more intervals, you increase the granularity of the statistical data which may help selectivity estimates for non-uniform data. However, the larger the number of intervals, the longer it may take to do query optimization.

SYSTEM MAXINTERVALS will use the system-determined number of intervals for this histogram.

These options are only valid when you specify a column or index explicitly.

USING MAXVALUELENGTH *n*
USING SYSTEM MAXVALUELENGTH

You can specify the maximum size for certain histogram values through USING MAXVALUELENGTH *n*, where *n* equals the number of CHARACTER or VARCHAR characters or the number of bytes for all other options.

For single columns, the valid range for *n* is 1 to the maximum size of the column. If you specify a larger size than the maximum size, the system will adjust the value down to the maximum size. The system will never truncate numeric values, and will increase the interval size to accommodate full values.

If you are collecting multicolumn statistics, the valid range for *n* is from 1 to the combined maximum size of the columns. The system concatenates the values and truncates them, if necessary, to fit the maximum size. If the maximum interval size would result in truncation of numeric data, the system will increase the interval to make room for the full numeric value.

Using the SYSTEM MAXVALUELENGTH option allows the system to use the pre-determined maximum value.

These options can only be used in conjunction with an explicit column or index statistic collection.

Enabling a Rollup

Consider the following statement.

```
COLLECT STATISTICS
 COLUMN (first_name, mgr_employee_no)
,COLUMN (first_name)
,COLUMN (mgr_employee_no)
ON employee_table;
```

Figure 16.5

Prior to TD14, the system would have done a full base table read for (first_name, mgr_employee_no), a second full base table read for (first_name), and a third full base table read for (mgr_employee_no).

With TD14, the system executes a full base table read for (first_name, mgr_employee_no) to perform the statistics multicolumn aggregation. It then performs a rollup for (first_name) from the prior multicolumn aggregation instead of reading the base table again. It then performs another rollup (mgr_employee_no) from the prior multicolumn aggregation instead of reading the base table again.

The following pages show the Explain of the COLLECT STATISTICS statement.

```
EXPLAIN
COLLECT STATISTICS
 COLUMN (first_name, mgr_employee_no)
,COLUMN (first_name)
,COLUMN (mgr_employee_no)
ON employee_table;
```

```
*** Help information returned. 53 rows.
*** Total elapsed time was 1 second.
```

```
Explanation
---------------------------------------------------------
  1) First, we lock CSQL_CLASS.employee_table for access.
  2) Next, we do an all-AMPs SUM step to aggregate from
     CSQL_CLASS.employee_table by way of an all-rows scan
     with no residual conditions , grouping by field1 (
     CSQL_CLASS.employee_table.First_name
     ,CSQL_CLASS.employee_table.Mgr_employee_no). Aggregate
     Intermediate Results are computed globally, then
     placed in Spool 18.  The size of Spool 18 is estimated
     with no confidence to be 7 rows (315 bytes).  The
     estimated time for this step is 0.05 seconds.
  3) Then we save the UPDATED STATISTICS for (
     'First_name,Mgr_employee_no') from Spool 18 into Spool
     4, which is built locally on a single AMP derived from
     the hash of the table id.
  4) We do an all-AMPs SUM step to aggregate from Spool 18
     by way of an all-rows scan , grouping by field1 (
     CSQL_CLASS.employee_table.First_name).  Aggregate
     Intermediate Results are computed globally, then
     placed in Spool 21.  The size of Spool 21 is estimated
     with no confidence to be 6 rows (198 bytes).  The
     estimated time for this step is 0.06 seconds.
  5) Then we save the UPDATED STATISTICS for ('First_name')
     from Spool 21 (Last Use) into Spool 9, which is built
     locally on a single AMP derived from the hash of the
     table id.
  6) We do an all-AMPs SUM step to aggregate from Spool 18
     (Last Use)by way of an all-rows scan , grouping by
     field1 (CSQL_CLASS.employee_table.Mgr_employee_no).
     Aggregate Intermediate Results are computed globally,
     then placed in Spool 24.  The size of Spool 24 is
     estimated with no confidence to be 5 rows (145 bytes).
     The estimated time for this step is 0.06 seconds.
  7) Then we save the UPDATED STATISTICS for
     ('Mgr_employee_no') from Spool 24 (Last Use) into
     Spool 14, which is built locally on a single AMP
     derived from the hash of the table id.
  8) We compute the table-level summary statistics from
     spool 14 and save them into Spool 16, which is built
     locally on a single AMP derived from the hash of the
     table id.
  9) We lock DBC.StatsTbl for write on a RowHash.
 10) We do a single-AMP ABORT test from DBC.StatsTbl by way
```

```
    of the primary index with a residual condition of (
    "((DBC.StatsTbl.ExpressionList = 'First_name') OR
    (DBC.StatsTbl.StatsId = 6 )) OR
    ((DBC.StatsTbl.ExpressionList =
    'First_name,Mgr_employee_no') OR (DBC.StatsTbl.StatsId
    = 5 ))").
11) We do a single-AMP MERGE into DBC.StatsTbl from Spool
    4 (Last Use).
12) We do a single-AMP MERGE into DBC.StatsTbl from Spool
    9 (Last Use).
13) We do a Single AMP MERGE Update to DBC.StatsTbl from
    Spool 14 (Last Use) by way of a RowHash match scan.
14) We do a Single AMP MERGE Update to DBC.StatsTbl from
    Spool 16 (Last Use) by way of a RowHash match scan.
15) We spoil the statistics cache for the table, view or
    query.
16) We spoil the parser's dictionary cache for the table.
17) Finally, we send out an END TRANSACTION step to all
    AMPs involved in processing the request.
 -> No rows are returned to the user as the result of
    statement 1.
```

Figure 16.6

COLLECT STATISTICS Examples

In the following example, notice the similarity of the CREATE INDEX and COLLECT STATISTICS commands:

```
CREATE INDEX (last_name, first_name) ON employee_table ;
COLLECT STATS INDEX (last_name, first_name) ON employee_table ;
```

Figure 16.7

The following are examples of collecting statistics on a column or column set:

```
COLLECT STATISTICS COLUMN dept_no ON employee_table ;
COLLECT STATISTICS COLUMN (dept_no, last_name) ON
employee_table ;
```

Figure 16.8

You can combine all of the above COLLECT STATS commands into one command, as shown below:

```
COLLECT STATISTICS
 INDEX (last_name, first_name)
, COLUMN dept_no
, COLUMN (dept_no, last_name)
ON employee_table ;
```

Figure 16.9

The following is an example of requesting sampling instead of a full table scan:

```
COLLECT STATISTICS USING SYSTEM SAMPLE COLUMN (dept_no,
last_name) ON employee_table ;
```

Figure 16.10

There are tradeoffs to consider when sampling a portion of a table instead of doing a full collection.

- The collection process doesn't take as long nor consume as many system resources.
- There is decreased confidence in the accuracy of the statistics.
- Using sampled statistics is better than relying on dynamic sampling or not having any statistics at all.

All existing statistics can be refreshed in a single command, by not specifying any INDEX or COLUMN entries, as shown below:

```
COLLECT STATISTICS ON employee_table ;
```

Figure 16.11

HELP STATISTICS Options

The HELP STATISTICS command, shown below, returns the following information:

- The DATE when statistics were last collected or refreshed.
- The TIME when statistics were last collected or refreshed.
- The count of UNIQUE VALUES.
- The COLUMN NAMES over which statistics were collected.

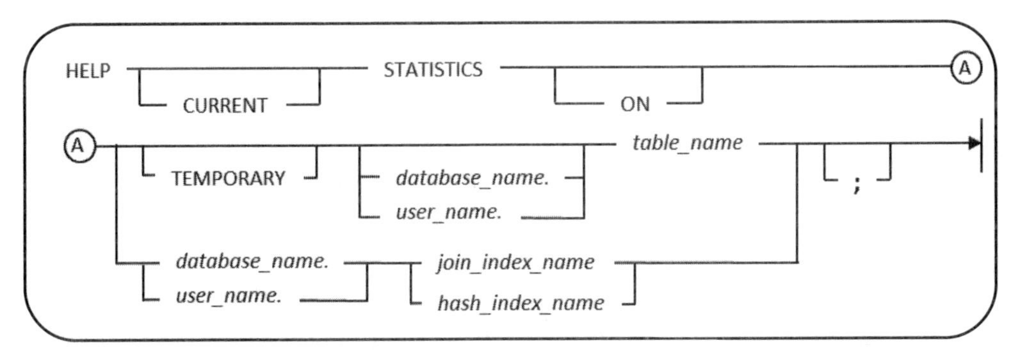

Figure 16.12

The date and time column are extremely useful. They assist you in determining when the statistics have been collected, refreshed, or even dropped.

Note: You can no longer specify a column or index for a HELP STATISTICS request. Also, you cannot display detailed statistics. HELP STATISTICS now reports only table-level summary statistics.

SHOW STATISTICS Command

With the new DBC.StatsTbl, activated in TD14, you can use the new SHOW STATISTICS command to view summary-level statistics (SHOW STATISTICS) or detail-level statistics (SHOW STATISTICS VALUES). You can also have the information returned in XML format which can be used as input to graphical displays, and other uses.

The following diagram is the syntax for the SHOW STATISTICS command.

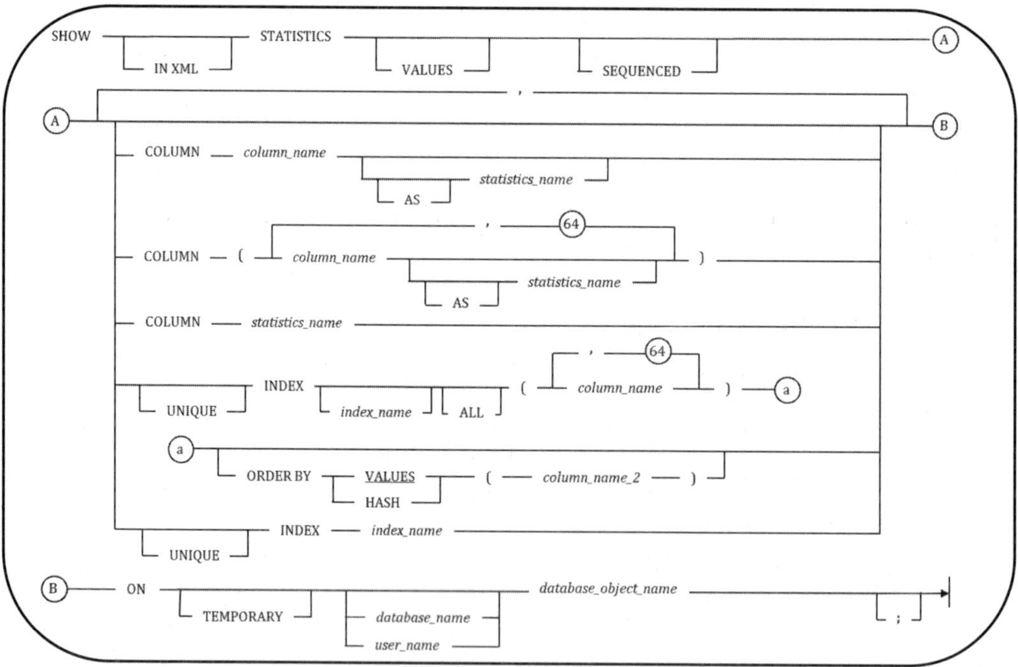

Figure 16.13

The following chart shows the difference between using the IN XML feature, and not using it.

SHOW IN XML STATISTICS...	The output can be used for transformations, advanced statistical processing, graphical displays, and the like.
SHOW STATISTICS...	The output can be used as a backup of the stats. They can be transferred to other system in the dual-active environments.

Figure 16.14

The VALUES option controls whether the system returns detailed statistics about all of the columns of the specified database object, unless you specify the columns and indexes you want.

The SUMMARY option reports just table-level stats.

The date, time, and timestamp data is always displayed in UTC format without conversion to the local time zone.

In addition, using standard SQL you can query DBC.StatsTbl using four new views:

- **DBC.ColumnStatsV** – statistics collected on individual indexed and non-indexed columns, including PARTITION statistics.
- **DBC.IndexStatsV** – statistics collected on indexes for which two or more columns have been defined.
- **DBC.MulticolumnStatsV** – statistics collected on groups of non-indexed columns.
- **DBC.TempTableStatsV** – statistics collected on the materialized temporary tables for the current session.

These new system views are not compatible with releases prior to Teradata Database 14.0. Furthermore, these new views do not return statistics information for row level security tables.

COLLECT STATISTICS - Recommendations

Here are some excellent guidelines on collecting statistics:

- **Non-unique Secondary Indices (NUSI):** It is very important to collect statistics on all NUSIs because this will impact whether or not the optimizer chooses to use the NUSI. If the NUSI is used in the ORDER BY command, it is important to collect statistics on this column. This will enable the optimizer to accurately compare the cost of using that index versus using a different access path.

- **Unique Primary Indices (UPI):** It is important to collect statistics on a UPI if the table is small (less than 100 rows per AMP) and if no other statistics are collected on that table. The only way the optimizer knows how many rows exist in the table is by collecting statistics on the primary index. Also, if there are multiple tables to be joined in a query, the optimizer can produce better join plans if you have PI statistics for each table.

- **Non-unique Primary Indices (NUPI):** Statistics should always be collected for the same reasons as above.

- **Join Indexes:** Statistics should be collected separately for base table columns and join index columns. The statistics for base tables and join indexes are not interchangeable, and the demographics for values in a base table are typically different from the join index values. Statistics for a join index should always be collected on the primary index column(s) of the join index. If there is a secondary index on the join index, then it is useful to collect statistics on the column(s) used to define that secondary index. In addition, it is a good practice to collect statistics on columns used as search conditions, columns used to join a join index with a table that is not part of the join index, and other popular join index columns, like those used frequently in WHERE conditions.

- **Hash Indexes:** Column statistics for single-table join indexes and hash indexes are often best collected directly on the base table columns rather than separately as is always required for multi-table join indexes.

- **Join Columns:** It is highly recommended to collect statistics on columns used in table joins. It is even more important to collect stats on columns involved in joining more than two tables. In addition, collect statistics on all columns of small reference tables used in joins. This will assist the optimizer in determining the best method and order for joining the tables together. Lastly, statistics helps the Optimizer to estimate with high confidence the spool file size required for the result set.

- **Partitioning Column:** This is the column(s) referenced in the PARTITION BY clause. Always collect statistics on:
    - PARTITION - Tells the optimizer how many partitions are empty and how many rows are in each partition. Used for optimizer costing.
    - The partitioning column. This provides cardinality estimates to the optimizer when the partitioning column is part of a query's selection criteria.

  Consider these statistics if the partitioning column is not part of the table's primary index (PI):
    - Most important when a given PI value may exist in multiple partitions.
    - Helps in costing sliding-window, rowkey join, dynamic partition elimination.
    - Can skip if PI value is contained within 1 partition.
    - Provides the combined number of distinct values for the combination of PI and partitioning columns after partition elimination.

  - Used in rowkey join costing.

- **Qualifying Columns** Any column used in a WHERE clause is a candidate for statistics collection. In particular, it is vital to collect statistics on columns containing highly skewed data. The reason for this is that when there are no statistics on a skewed column, the optimizer chooses to take a conservative course by assuming that a certain percentage of the data values will qualify for the query.

You can collect statistics on a group of non-indexed columns. Collecting statistics on a group of columns allows the Optimizer to better estimate the number of rows required to complete queries.

This feature saves overhead cost because you no longer have to use a secondary index in order to collect statistics on a group of columns. The benefits here are space savings and I/O overhead because secondary indexes are not needed for just that purpose.

The recommendation is to collect statistics on a group of non-indexed columns is based on the following:

- They appear frequently together in query selection conditions.
- A secondary index is defined solely to allow statistics collection and is never used for indexed data access.
- The Optimizer's row estimate in the EXPLAIN output is incorrect which results in a bad query plan. Collecting stats on the group of columns in this query can definitely improve performance.

To ensure the best query plans, consider collecting statistics on the following, more general set of table columns:

- All indexes.
- High-access join columns.

- Non-indexed columns frequently referenced in WHERE clause predicates, particularly if those columns contain skewed data.
- The partitioning column set of a PPI table.
- The system-defined PARTITION column for all tables, both PPI *and* NPPI.

Note: Accurate statistics can make the difference between a successful query and a query that runs out of spool space. It is recommended to recollect when 10% or greater of the data changes. In addition if the Partitioning column changes by greater than 10% by itself it should be recollected.

Statistics Wizard

The principal focus of query tuning is to provide reliable summary information about the data to the Optimizer. This is done by collecting accurate statistics, which are then stored in a synoptic data structure known as an interval histogram. The correct choice of the column and index sets on which statistics should be collected can help the Optimizer generate better query plans, dramatically improving query performance, and reducing the collection overhead. It can be difficult to understand how the Optimizer uses statistics, to decide what statistics are needed, without an automated method to recommend them. That automated method is the Teradata Statistics Wizard, which is a client-based GUI interface for obtaining statistics recommendations for particular queries or query workloads submitted to it for analysis.

Teradata Statistics Wizard is a graphical tool that can improve the performance of queries and, as a result, the entire Teradata Database. It reduces the time to collect data and eliminates the need for constant customizing.

Statistics Wizard accomplishes this by automating the process of collecting statistics for a particular workload or selecting arbitrary indexes or columns for collection/re-collection purposes. Additionally, validate the proposed statistics on a production system to verify the performance of the proposed statistics before applying the recommendations.

Statistics Wizard enables the DBA to:

- Review the statistics suggestions but does not add all the statements without testing.
- Identify single-column high confidence columns and missing system-derived column PARTITION statistics.
- Specify a workload to be analyzed for recommendations specific to improving the performance of the queries in a workload.
- Select an arbitrary database or selection of tables, indexes, or columns for analysis, collection, or re-collection of statistics.
- Make recommendations, based on a specific workload.
- Make recommendations, based on table demographics and general heuristics.
- Defer executing the collection and dropping of statistics and schedule for a later time.
- Display and modify the interval statistics for a column or index.

As changes are made within a database, Statistics Wizard identifies those changes and recommends which tables should have statistics collected, based on age of data and table growth, and which columns/indexes would benefit from having statistics defined and collected for a specific workload. The DBA is then given the opportunity to accept or reject the recommendations.

- The Teradata Statistics Wizard client utility can determine which indexes best support a join index for a specified SQL query workload.
- The Teradata Index Wizard client can determine optimum secondary indexes for particular SQL workloads.

- The Teradata Statistics Wizard utility does *not* support hash indexes.

In particular, the Teradata Statistics Wizard can use database query log information to analyze SQL workloads for determining recommendations for collecting statistics on particular tables, columns, and indexes.

Chapter 16: Practice Questions

1. Which data dictionary tables are used to store statistics? (Choose 2)
    a. DBC.TVM
    b. DBC.Indexes
    c. DBC.StatsTbl
    d. DBC.Stats
    e. DBC.Dbase

2. Sample statistics is recommended for ______________.
    a. Large tables
    b. Highly skewed data
    c. Small tables
    d. Replacing all full scan collections

3. How many full table scans will the system do of table t1 to accomplish the following statistics collection?

    ```
    COLLECT STATISTICS
    COLUMN (c1, c2, c3, c4), COLUMN (c1, c2), COLUMN (c3),
    COLUMN (c1, c4), COLUMN (C3, C4) ON t1;
    ```

    a. 1
    b. 2
    c. 3
    d. 4
    e. 5

4. Which of the following HELP commands is valid?
    a. HELP STATISTICS t4 COLUMN (c2, c5);
    b. HELP CURRENT STATISTICS ON TEMPORARY t1;
    c. HELP TEMPORARY STATISTICS t1;
    d. HELP STATISTICS t7 INDEX (C3, C4);

5. Which of the following views are valid with TD14.0? (Choose 2)
    a. DBC.ColumnStats
    b. DBC.ColumnStatsV
    c. DBC.IndexStats
    d. DBC.IndexStatsV
    e. DBC.MultiColumnStats

Chapter Notes

Utilize this space for notes, key points to remember, diagrams, areas of further study, etc.

Appendix

Answers to the Chapter Practice Questions

CHAPTER 2	CHAPTER 3	CHAPTER 4	CHAPTER 5	CHAPTER 6
1. b, d, e 2. c 3. c 4. 6, 5, 2, 4, 1, 3 5. a	1. a 2. b 3. d 4. b 5. c	1. b, e 2. c, e 3. h+i f+j h+k g+j f+k 4. b 5. a	1. b 2. c 3. a 4. b	1. a, e 2. c 3. b 4. All All All 2 All 1

CHAPTER 7	CHAPTER 8	CHAPTER 9	CHAPTER 10	CHAPTER 11
1. b 2. e 3. Spool Perm Perm Temp Spool	1. e 2. d 3. e 4. a	1. d 2. a, e 3. a, d 4. b 5. c 6. e	1. c 2. d, e 3. b 4. c 5. b	1. e 2. d 3. c, e 4. c 5. d

CHAPTER 12	CHAPTER 13	CHAPTER 14	CHAPTER 15	CHAPTER 16
1. c 2. b 3. d 4. a 5. a, d	1. c 2. b 3. b 4. d 5. d 6. b	1. b 2. c 3. b 4. c 5. d	1. a 2. b 3. c 4. e 5. d, e	1. b, c 2. a 3. a 4. b 5. b, d

INDEX

G

H

I

J

L

M

N

O

P

Q

R

S

T

U

V